A Season of Prayers

Peppi Cooper

authorHOUSE®

AuthorHouse™
1663 Liberty Drive
Bloomington, IN 47403
www.authorhouse.com
Phone: 1 (800) 839-8640

Published by AuthorHouse 10/24/2018

ISBN: 978-1-5462-5745-5 (sc)
ISBN: 978-1-5462-5744-8 (e)

Library of Congress Control Number: 2018910158

Print information available on the last page.

DEDICATION

This book is dedicated to my family and the softball players, coaches, fans, and family members who have touched my life. While these prayers were prayed over the Auburn Softball and Team USA players and coaches, those names could be substituted for any program anywhere. I believe that our heavenly Father goes with us wherever we go--- including a softball field and that He teaches lessons through the trials and tribulations faced through the game of softball. In some cases, the odds were so great against Auburn that only God's intervention saw them through. I hope you enjoy reading these prayers as much as I enjoyed praying them, and may these prayers be forever as incense in front of our Heavenly Father.

Jan 08, 2015 5:36am

This shout out is for the Auburn softball team as they go through hell week. "You are braver than you believe, and stronger than you seem, and smarter than you think." Christopher Robin to Winnie the Pooh

War Eagle

Feb 22, 2015 7:51am

It's a great day for Auburn softball;) Blessed to be cheering on my daughter, her teammates, and their coaches! Counting my blessings today---still counting-----still counting----still counting... "This is the day the Lord hath made; I will rejoice and be glad in it."

My Prayer

"Lord, please give these young women confidence in themselves with every play. Keep them and their coaches safe both on and off the field. Keep them under Your wings of protection so that anyone who sees them, talks to them, has contact with them, or talks about them will have Christ in his or her heart." Amen and War Eagle

Feb 27, 2015 5:37am

Guess What? We get to watch the Auburn Tiger Softball team play against Ohio State tonight at 5 p.m. Bundle Up! It's going to be cold. My prayer for today, "Lord, thank you for Your vigilance in keeping these young ladies, their coaches, and their support staff safe. Thank you for giving these young ladies Coach Myers and his sons to teach and guide them both on and off the field. Help these players submit to their leadership so that they can learn the life lessons You want them to be taught. Thank You for the second, third, fourth, fifth…infinite chances that you provide for us to learn the lessons that we must learn before we can advance to the next base. Softball is a small part of what these young ladies do, and I thank You for using it to season them for the bigger Game of Life. Thank you for putting coaches in their lives who believe in them and who put them back in the game after mistakes so that they can conquer the challenges You allow in their lives. Let others see YOU in how the coaches coach and in how the players play. Thank you for being my Coach and theirs. Please help these young ladies see and feel Your love today and always." Amen and War Eagle

Feb 28, 2015 2:14pm

Happy Game Day:) Today is Strike Out Cancer Day---remember to wear PINK! My family, like many others has been touched in some way by breast cancer. I've noticed that those who are fighting cancer and those who have fought cancer have three things in common. They are tenacious; they fight like champions; and they are part of a sisterhood.

Today's Prayer

"Father, thank you for wrapping Your loving arms around those who are battling with breast cancer and for filling them with the courage to fight. You promise us that You will heal us, and I'm asking You to give faith to those who are in the midst of battling this disease and for You to heal them. Thank you for my daughters' health, and for the health of Kasey's teammates, and coaches. Let both teams today FIGHT LIKE GIRLS in honor of those who have fought cancer and for those who are fighting cancer right now." Amen and War Eagle

Mar 01, 2015 9:26am

Happy Sunday and Happy Game Day

Today's Prayer

"Thank you Father for the Fellowship of Christian Athletes and the chaplains that are available to minister to these young ladies on Sundays and any other day. Thank you for the words of wisdom that You wrote for us in Ephesians 6:10-17 telling us to arm ourselves with Your armor. Metaphorically, we'd look like a catcher--because we're covered from head to toe. Around our loins, we have Truth. Around our chest, we have Righteousness. On our feet, we have the Gospel of Peace. For a shield, we have Faith. On our heads, we have Salvation. And we defend ourselves with the Sword of the Spirit. Thank you for giving us the tools we need to arm ourselves for the spiritual wars we will face. Keep these young ladies safe today, and draw them to You so that they will be armed in Your armor." Amen and War Eagle

Mar 04, 2015 7:03am

Happy Travel Day

"Lord, please keep these young ladies, their coaches, their support staff, and their families safe as they make their way to Fullerton, California. Clear their path, so that there are no lines, no unexpected interruptions, no forgotten luggage, and only friendly people in their path. May those who see them, talk to them, think about them, or talk about them have You in their hearts." Amen

Mar 05, 2015 9:49am

Game Day Prayer

"Dear Lord,

Thank you for safe travels yesterday for the Auburn softball family. Thank you for the beautiful California weather and for the opportunity to meet and to play teams from the West Coast. Give our players and coaches the quiet confidence and inner strength that only You can give, and help other teams and fans to see Your goodness and greatness in these young ladies, their coaches, their support staff, and their families. Make Your greatness so obvious that others have to ask, 'What's different about this team?,' and we can honor You with the answer-- You are the difference." Amen.

Mar 06, 2015 9:50am

Oh, Happy Day! We're celebrating a birthday in the Cooper household today...And where will we be? At the ball park, of course.

Game Day Prayer

"Lord, thank you for keeping these players, their coaches, their support staff, and their families in the palm of Your hands throughout this trip. Thank you for the challenges You put into these young ladies' lives through softball. Lord, thank you for being the most patient Coach there is, and help these young ladies to realize that You will put them in the same situation over and over again until the lesson they are supposed to learn is learned. Lord, We accept Your Coaching, and thank you for loving us." Amen

Mar 07, 2015 8:58am

Happy Saturday! And I accept Susan Gatlin's challenge to post a scripture for 7 days. Here we go, "I can do all things through Christ who strengthens me." Philippians 4:13. And...here goes our Game Day Prayer

"Thank you, Father for Your continued grace during this trip. Thank you for putting us on our backs so that the only place we can look is UP and to You so that You will be the only answer for our troubles. Thank you for equipping us with all that we need through Christ. Keep these young ladies safe today as we go into our last game of the series. Help others to see Your greatness in us. Fill us up." Amen.

Mar 08, 2015 5:10am

Happy Sunday and Travel Day!

"Lord, thank you for a wonderful time in California. Now, it's time to go back to sweet home Auburn and Dothan, Alabama, and East Lansing, Michigan. Please keep these young ladies, their coaches, their support staff, and families safe as they travel back home. May everyone who crosses their path have You in their hearts. Clear any obstacles that may come their way so that they will all be safely home later today. Thank you for the lessons You taught all of us this week." Amen

Mar 11, 2015 8:22pm

Great night for softball.

Game Day Prayer

"Thank you, Lord, for the opportunity to see Auburn play tonight and for the chance to see former Patriots on the Troy team. Lord, please give these players, their coaches, and families safe travel tonight. And help these young ladies learn from tonight's game as their coaches prepare them for SEC play." Amen and War Eagle

Mar 12, 2015 5:39am

Softball Prayer

"Lord, please help each player on the Auburn softball team get 1% better in one skill set today. Fielders---1% better at fielding a ball to their weak side--- Pitchers---1% better with their best pitch; Hitters--1% better with their pitch selection--- Catchers---1% better with their communication. If we get 1% better each day we are on the field, we'll be 168% better fielders, pitchers, and hitters at the end of the season." Amen and War Eagle

Mar 13, 2015 6:10am

Travel Day Prayer

"Lord, I realize that You are not a vending machine, and when I need something, I go up to the machine, make my selection, pray, and poof, my prayer is answered. So, today, I want to praise You and thank You for all the blessings in my life and in the lives of my family and in my extended Auburn softball and work families' lives. Thank you for Your mercy. Thank You for sending Your angels to watch over us and to be a buffer between us and anything that might harm us. Thank You for allowing us to come to You with every care and need that we have. You are a mighty God, and we are Your children. Thank You for my answered prayers and my unanswered prayers. You know what we need, and I know that You will provide for Your children abundantly." Amen

Mar 14, 2015 6:23am

It's SEC opening day for Auburn softball.

Game Day Prayer

"Lord, thank you for the blessings of safe travel and good health. Thank you for the coaches, support staff, and families that You have put in the lives of these young ladies to mentor them, to teach them, and to shape their mental approach to the game to one of discipline. Help these young ladies to play with a purpose and to play aligned as a team. If they will, there is no limit to where they can go. Help them to honor You in all that they do and to recognize that You gave them a physical gift and that they are to use that gift to bring glory to You." Amen and War Eagle

Mar 15, 2015 9:08am

Happy Sunday and Hello SUNSHINE:! Today...may be one of the few days that we have played with the sun shining.

Game Day Prayer

"Lord, thank You for the rain and cold because without them, we wouldn't celebrate the sun and heat. Thank you for continuing to keep our players healthy. Thank you for their continued success. Help them to understand that every victory is preparing them for the next challenge. Your lessons aren't, 'One and Done.' We are supposed to remember the lessons You teach us. You build on our successes and teach us in our battles. Thank You for equipping our players and coaches with the mental tools and physical gifts they need to play this great sport. Keep both teams safe throughout this series, and help us (players, coaches, support staff, fans, and parents) to honor You in all that we do today." Amen and War Eagle

Mar 16, 2015 5:35am

Happy Monday! Our Tigers play tonight at 6 on the SEC network.

Game Day Prayer

"Lord, thank you for keeping all of our players and coaches safe thus far in this series. Thank you for giving our players the courage to play in front of folks who were yelling and screaming at them in ways that did not show sportsmanship, and thank you for intervening. Thank you for intervening in our lives in ways such that we never know...we just know that something 'Stopped.' Please continue to give these young ladies the courage to do the right thing and to turn the other cheek. Not only were they yelled at, Jade was hit twice. Thank you for giving her discipline. Thank you for the lessons You have taught these young ladies thus far and for the ones that are yet to come. Thank you for helping these young ladies honor You in their actions. Please continue to keep these young ladies safe, and give them, their coaches, fans, and parents safe travels tonight as they return to Auburn." Amen and War Eagle

Mar 16, 2015 8:30pm

Great night for a sweep:) War Eagle.

"Lord, thank you for keeping our players, coaches, support staff, families, and fans safe throughout this series. Please clear their path for safe travels back to Auburn or to their homes." Amen and War Eagle

Mar 20, 2015 5:37am

Hello Kentucky, welcome to the Plains. First---thank you to the Auburn Family for showing Southern hospitality to the Kentucky players and coaching staff. That's what it is supposed to look like.

Game Day Prayer

"Lord, thank you so much for the Auburn coaching staff and players. Thank you for the leadership and sportsmanship they display before and during games. Please help us to remember to treat others the way we want to be treated. Sometimes we slip, but thank You for giving us the nudge to get back on the right track. Throughout this series, help these young ladies to play to their potential. Help them to share with each other how the pitcher is pitching and to give a heads up to their teammates when Kentucky players are trying to bunt or steal. Help our fielders to communicate with each other when the ball is coming their way and to shout out where the ball needs to be thrown next. Help these young ladies to play with the skills You have given them, and help them to get better with every pitch and every play. Thank you for the safe travels to Kentucky, and thank you for the angels You are placing in front of, behind, beside, above, and below these players to keep them safe. Thank you for preparing these young ladies for today. Help our players and coaches to play the game One pitch at a time and One play at a time for 21 outs." Amen and War Eagle

Mar 20, 2015 9:37pm

Great Win for the Auburn Softball Team. Go Tigers... ready for a double header tomorrow.

Prayer

"Lord, we are to praise You for all things. Thank you for the win, and please heal three of our players. You know who they are." Amen and War Eagle

Mar 21, 2015 11:16am

It's Game Day! Game Day Prayer

"Lord, thank you for the blessings of today. It's beautiful. The families are enjoying each other. The players are smiling. The players and coaches are prepared, and we are looking forward to using the gifts that You have given us to honor You today. Thank you for having a doctor in just the right place at just the right time last night. I see Your intervention every day, and I praise You for it. You tell us, 'You have not because you ask not.' I'm boldly coming to Your thrown to ask for Your continued blessings on these players, their coaches, support staff, and the families of both the players and coaches. Help us to see Your hand in our lives. Please help our players to only hear what they are supposed to hear today, to focus only on what they are supposed to focus on today, and to forget about yesterday. We are to live for today-it is Your gift to us. Help us to live in the moments You are giving to us." Amen and War Eagle

Mar 21, 2015 10:06pm

Go Tigers:) Clean Sweep of Kentucky. Very proud of these young ladies for helping each other and playing as a team.

"Thank you, Lord, for showing us our weaknesses so that we can learn from them. Thank you for helping these young ladies stare adversity in the face and walk right through it. I know You are preparing them for the adversity they will face not only in softball, but in the bigger game of life. Thank you for keeping them safe throughout this series. Please give all safe travels home." Amen and War Eagle

Mar 25, 2015 5:59am

It's going to be a beautiful day for a softball game... Auburn vs. Florida State.

Game Day Prayer

"Thank you, Lord, for safe travels and for Your continued grace and mercy with these players, coaches, support staff, families, and fans. Help our players and coaches approach this game with courage and strength. Keep our players and coaches safe and healthy throughout this series. Continue to heal those who are touched with sickness. We know that the devil has a way of throwing us a curve ball, and we are thankful that You are in charge. Help these young ladies to have the courage to stand up to the curve balls they are thrown and say, 'Enough! In the name of Jesus ... GO back to where you came from.' Help us all to realize that when You are for us, no one or nothing else stands a chance. Thank you for Your promise to never forsake us, and thank you for being our biggest Fan." Amen and War Eagle

Mar 26, 2015 5:35am

Travel Day Prayer

"Lord, please keep our players, coaches, support staff, fans, and parents safe as they travel to Columbia, MO. Clear their path so that they have a quick flight without complications. Put angels in front of them, behind them, underneath them, above them, below them, and beside them to protect them. May all who see them, talk to them, talk about them, hear them, or think about them have You in their hearts. Give them rest when they get to Columbia. Clear their minds so that they can focus on all the good things they have learned and the progress they are making as a team.

Continue to heal those who are touched with injury or sickness, and give them hope and courage to overcome these setbacks. I say *setbacks* because You tell us that if we have just the faith of a mustard seed, we can move mountains. Please, give these young ladies FAITH. I'm claiming healing on their behalf until they are mature enough to claim healing for themselves. Thank you for being the Master Physician. Thank you for the work that I see You doing in all of our lives." Amen and War Eagle

Mar 27, 2015 6:23am

Game Day Prayer

"Dear Lord,

Thank you for our safe travels and for the blessings You have showered down on these young ladies, coaches, coaching staff, parents, and fans. Often, we don't say, 'Thank you,' until we are shown what our lives 'could be.' Help us to realize that everything we do and that everything we can ever hope to do is because of You. Thank you for the lessons of Wed. night and for the opportunity to grow as a team. Help these young ladies to realize that when circumstances in their lives are tough, they are living their testimonies. One day, they will say, 'Do you remember that game against.. .?' Or 'Do you remember when ... ?' Or someone will ask them, 'Has xyz ever happened to you?' And they will be able to say, 'Yes. One day .. .' Or, 'Let me tell you a story.' Thank you for our lessons and for our testimony. During this series, help our testimony to be worthy of You. Help others to see Your hand on these young ladies. Help them to play to their potential, to play in the moment, and to play as a team. Help them to play to their own strengths, and to recognize the weaknesses of their teammates and to adjust their actions accordingly so that there are no weaknesses--only strengths." Amen and War Eagle

Mar 27, 2015 11:50pm

Saturday Game Day Prayer

"Lord, thank you for keeping these young ladies safe during Friday's game. Today, help them to be students of the game. Help them to learn with every pitch and to keep moving forward. Help them to play one pitch at a time, one catch at a time, one throw at a time, one hit at a time, as one team.--One pitch, one play, one team--ONE. Help those who are learning lessons---as You are a Master Teacher, to look UP, and to realize that sometimes, You put them in situations so that they only place they can go is to their knees, so that they will turn to You and look UP. You will lift them up on eagles' wings. You know who they are, and I praise You for the lessons You are teaching them." Amen and War Eagle

Mar 29, 2015 8:05am

Game Day Prayer

"Lord, thank you for answered and unanswered prayers--because You know what we need better than we do. Please reach down and fill the heartache of loss with the hope of a win. Your rewards are right on time and not on our personal time tables. Ezra 10:4 states, 'Rise up. This matter is in your hands. We will support you, so take courage and do it.' There is nothing that the parents, coaches, support staff, fans, and players wouldn't do for these players, but there are some things that our players have to do on their own. Today is that day. Help the players realize they are not alone. Help them hear, see, and feel the cheerleaders that all around them--in the dugout, on the sidelines, in the stands, and in front of the televisions in homes across the country. Today, give these young women courage. Give each pitcher the courage to throw the pitch that is called with confidence; give each batter the courage to hit her best pitch; give each fielder the courage to go get those balls and trust her throws; give the catchers the courage to take charge and lead from behind the plate; give each runner the courage to run; give the dugout the courage to shout out when the batters are about to bunt or steal; give the coaches the courage to coach. ...from Galatians 6:9..'Let us not become weary in doing good for at the proper time, we will reap a harvest if we do not give up.' Thank you for being right on time." Amen and War Eagle

Apr 02, 2015 3:11pm

Game Day Prayer

"Dear Lord,

Thank you for the blessings You have showered onto the Auburn softball players, coaches, support staff, and families. Thank you for the hope that we have because Your Son died on the cross. He conquered death, and You promise us that we can do ALL things and conquer all things because we are Your children. Thank You for Your Son. During this series, remind our players that they can do ALL things through You. Fill in their weaknesses with the strengths of their teammates and with Your power and love. Help them to draw on Your strength when they feel weak. Thank you for always keeping Your promises to us. And thank you for the promises that will be fulfilled because of the price that was paid for us 2015 years ago tomorrow." Amen and War Eagle

Apr 03, 2015 6:49am

Game Day Prayer

"Dear Lord,

Today, 2,015 years ago, You died on the cross for our sins. You conquered death, and Your blood covered our sins, the sins of our children, and the sins of our children's children. Thank you for the price You paid for us. You are a God of Hope and Victory. Help our players, coaches, support staff, fans, and parents take a moment today to remember You and the price that You paid for us because of Your love for us. Help our team to remember that the greatest gift we can ever have is love. In fact, You command us to love one another. Help our team to feel Your love and the love that we have for them as parents, coaches, teammates, and fans. Love can conquer anything because there is nothing--even death--that we won't do for each other if we truly know the meaning of LOVE." Amen and War Eagle

Apr 04, 2015 10:47am

Game Day Prayer

"Dear Lord,

Thank you for answered prayers. I prayed that our players would feel Your love and the love of the coaches, parents, other players, support staff, and fans yesterday, and for the first time this year, the stadium sold out last night--and today's game is sold out too. You are a mighty God. Please continue to let our players feel Your love. Help them play to their full potential today." Amen and War Eagle

Apr 08, 2015 11:47am

Game Day Prayer

"Dear Lord,

Thank you for the blessings of today. Help our players and coaches build on the successes and lessons they have experienced over this season as they play tonight. Help them see Your hand on their lives today and always. Walk beside them, and be their strength in their weakness." Amen and War Eagle

Apr 09, 2015 7:05am

Travel Day Prayer

"Lord, please be with the Auburn Softball family as they travel to College Station today. Send angels to clear their path and to keep them safe. May everyone who sees them, talks to them, thinks about them, or hears them have You in their heart." Amen and War Eagle

Apr 09, 2015 9:21am

Thought for the day.

God is never silent to our prayers or blind to our tears. He sees our tears, hears our prayers, and He will Deliver.

Apr 10, 2015 9:14am

Game Day Prayer

"Dear Lord,

Thank you for safe travels yesterday. Thank you for always delivering on time. Give our players the courage to deliver. Sometimes they may need a little push, which comes from circumstances You place in their path. Help them to recognize adversity as an opportunity, and continue to give them the inner strength to Step Up. They can do great things through You. Please walk beside them through this series." Amen and War Eagle

Apr 11, 2015 8:14am

Game Day Prayer

"Dear Lord,

Thank you for keeping our players, coaches, support staff, and families safe on and off the field. Continue to walk beside them, and send your angels to clear their path. Thank you for the physical gifts You have given these young ladies. Help them to use their gifts to honor You today and always." Amen and War Eagle

Apr 15, 2015 12:00pm

Travel and Game Day Prayer

"Lord, thank you for being Bigger than anything we can ever dream of facing. Thank you for continuing to pour blessings on these young ladies, coaches, support staff, families, and fans. Please be with them as they travel to and from Birmingham today. Keep them under Your protection, and raise them up on eagles' wings. Please help them to appreciate that one unfocused moment can change their lives and the lives of those who love them forever. Help them to keep their focus today. Help our players honor You with the gifts You have given them. Thank you for restoring our players' health, and I ask that you heal the Alabama pitcher who was hit in the chest last night." Amen and War Eagle

Apr 17, 2015 5:50am

Game Day Prayer

"Dear Lord,

Thank you for the rain. You know what our farmers need, and we praise You for it. This is a chaotic weekend for the Auburn sports family. Please help all of us to be mindful that we are hosts and hostesses for thousands this weekend, and our behavior will be on display for the entire country and for You. Please keep the players, coaches, support staff, families, and fans for both Auburn and the visiting team safe. Help our players to play to their full potential and to honor You with the physical gifts You gave them. I know that You are the biggest cheerleader that both teams have, and I pray that the games will be pleasing to You. Let our thoughts, words, and actions please You today and always. Help us to be wonderful hosts and hostesses to our visitors." Amen and War Eagle

Apr 18, 2015 7:44am

Game Day Prayer

"Lord, we are to praise You in everything. Thank you for the lessons You are teaching our players and coaches. You are the most patient Coach in the universe, and You will put us in the same situations over and over again until the lesson is learned. Help us to learn our lessons quickly today. Thank you for keeping both teams safe last night and for the sportsmanship everyone displayed. Help our players to push through today, and help them to realize that they can do all things through You." Amen and War Eagle

Apr 24, 2015 3:48pm

Game Day Prayer

"Dear Lord,

Thank you for blessings of today. Thank you for the three seniors on our team: Branndi Melero; Morgan Estell; and Mackinzie Kilpatrick and for the leadership they have provided to their teammates. Thank you for giving us a chance to celebrate them this weekend. Keep us safe, and may all the players, coaches, fans, and parents say, think, and do bring honor to You." Amen and War Eagle

Apr 25, 2015 2:00pm

Game Day Prayer

"Dear Lord,

Thank you for the gift of today! Help us to live all 86,400 seconds of today. Yesterday is gone; tomorrow is not promised; so, we are left with today. Please be with our players, coaches, fans, and parents today. Walk beside all of us. Help our players take what they have learned in practice and from their previous games with them today so that they can learn new lessons. Set our players apart so that they will get a chance to talk about You in their testimony. Let softball be an avenue for them to bring honor to You." Amen and War Eagle

Apr 26, 2015 7:54am

Game Day Prayer

"Lord,

Thank you for keeping everyone safe in Dothan and the surrounding areas yesterday through the storm. Thank you for having the final say for anything the enemy sends our way. Today, as we celebrate the three seniors on Auburn's team, let them enjoy the fruits of their labor. Continue to keep the Auburn softball family safe, and may all that our players, coaches, fans, and parents say, think, and do bring honor to You." Amen and War Eagle

Apr 30, 2015 5:39am

Travel Day Prayer

"Dear Lord, thank you for the blessings You continue to bring into our lives. Keep the Auburn softball family safe as they make their way to Baton Rouge. Put angels beside them, over them, beneath them, and behind them to protect them. May anyone who sees them, thinks of them, hears them, talks to them, or talks about them have You in their heart. May our softball family have opportunities to show the world that You are their strength." Amen and War Eagle

May 01, 2015 8:14am

Game Day Prayer

"Dear Lord,

Thank you for keeping the Auburn softball family safe. As our players go into this series, help them model the discipline and skills that their coaches have been teaching and grooming them for since last year. All of them----coaches and players-----have been working towards this weekend since the first workout of the year. May they reap the fruit of their labor 10 fold." Amen and War Eagle

May 02, 2015 10:35am

Game Day Prayer

"Dear Lord,

Thank you for keeping our players safe in last night's game. Thank you for the grace and sportsmanship they showed throughout the game. Continue to help clear their minds so that they can prepare for their final exams. Help the lessons they have learned come freely to them when they sit for their exams and as they put on their uniforms and step onto the field to play LSU. May others continue to see Your hand on their lives and in their actions both on and off the field. May their actions bring others to You." Amen and War Eagle

May 03, 2015 11:12am

Game Day Prayer

"Dear Lord,

Thank you for blessing the Auburn softball players, coaches, families, and fans. Thank you for the hospitality the Auburn family has been shown at the hotel. Help that hospitality carry over to Tiger stadium today and throughout the SEC tournament. Please let our players and coaches begin to harvest the seeds that were sewn last year. Let the extended Auburn softball family be a blessing to others today, and let our actions bring honor and glory to You." Amen and War Eagle

May 07, 2015 6:18am

Game Day Prayer

"Dear Lord,

Thank you for the journey You have provided these young ladies and their coaches. I believe You have answered my prayers and the prayers of others, and I praise You for it. As these young ladies and coaches begin the last phase of this year's journey, let them start with a clean slate, a clear mind, a winner's attitude, and confidence. May they demonstrate the lessons You have taught them, and may they carry over the lessons from practice to the playing field. Keep them safe, and set their level of play above their own abilities so that it is clear to those who watch them that they are Your children. May softball be a platform for them to honor You and to bring others to You." Amen and War Eagle

May 07, 2015 6:38am

Game Day Prayer

"Dear Lord,

Thank you for the blessings You have poured down on these young ladies and their coaches. Thank you for the lessons You have taught them on their journey this year and for the lessons yet to be taught. I believe You have answered my prayers and the prayers of others and I praise You for it. As they go into post season play, please be with them. Help them to carry the lessons they have learned into this part of their journey. Help them to play above their ability so that it is clear that You are providing their strength. Clear their minds, and give them the quiet confidence and calmness that only You can give. May softball be a platform for them to bring honor to You and others to Your thrown." Amen and War Eagle

May 07, 2015 8:36pm

Congratulations to the Auburn Tigers on your win today. One pitch, one at bat, one play at a time--- on your way to OKC.

May 08, 2015 5:48am

Game Day Prayer

"Dear Lord,

Thank you for second chances. You are the most patient Teacher and Coach. You put us in the same situations until we learn the lesson we are to learn. Today is a second chance day. Help our players and coaches push through with the lessons they have learned when...they find themselves up to bat with two outs, two strikes, and runners in scoring position, or when that curve ball isn't breaking the way it should break, or when they have to run like a gazelle to track down a ball or dive to catch a line drive or a grounder, help our players' self-talk to be one of the promises that You taught us to say, 'I can do all things through Christ who strengthens me.' Give our players faith that they can do Anything as long as You are first in their lives. Thank you for keeping Your promises." Amen and War Eagle

May 08, 2015 4:27pm

Congratulations to the Auburn Tigers in your win against Alabama! I am so proud of all of you. "Thank you, Lord, for being a God of firsts." Welcome to the SEC Winners' circle! Amen and War Eagle

May 09, 2015 6:49am

Game Day Prayer

"Dear Lord,

Thank you for taking care of the details for us. Thank you for taking our players to places they have never been before. Today, help them to stay focused on the prize. Keep both teams safe, and let our players play above their abilities. Help others to know that there is something special about these young ladies. Give them a quiet confidence today and a sense of calmness. Let softball be a platform for bringing others to You, and may all that the players, coaches, fans, and parents do bring honor to You." Amen and War Eagle

May 11, 2015 5:38am

Monday Morning Prayer

"Dear Lord,

Thank you for being a God of Firsts in the lives of the Auburn softball players' and coaches' lives. Thank you for allowing the entire world to witness the firsts in the last 48 hours---First time the players made it to the SEC final game; First SEC softball championship in school history; and First time Auburn will host Regionals and Super Regionals. May our players and coaches continue to honor You and to be a witness for You today and always." Amen and War Eagle

May 15, 2015 5:02am

Game Day Prayer

"Dear Lord,

Thank you for Your love and for the love the Auburn family has for the Auburn softball players and coaches. Help our players continue to be students of the game by getting a little bit smarter with every pitch that is thrown. Place filters on their ears so that they only hear cheers and words of encouragement. Help them to play above their ability so that it is clear to anyone who watches them that You have Your hand on their lives not only in softball but in everything they do. Give them a sense of calmness and peace that only You can bring. Please put angels around players from all of the teams so that they stay injury free. May all that the players, coaches, parents, and fans do bring honor to You. Thank you for all that You have done for us and for these young ladies." Amen and War Eagle

May 16, 2015 7:56am

Game Day Prayer

"Dear Lord,

Thank you for allowing our players to be successful last night. Let all of the players, coaches, parents, and fans be encouragers of each other throughout this series. Help them to understand that success is a journey. Thank you for all of the players and coaches. Each has a special purpose. Let all of them fulfill their purpose today and always. Let softball be a road for us to bring others to You." Amen and War Eagle

May 17, 2015 7:42am

Game Day Prayer

"Dear Lord,

Thank you for the blessings You continue to shower upon our players and coaches. I can see Your favor on this program. Today, fill them up with the confidence and joy they have had since they were on a t-ball field during opening ceremonies and with the excitement of getting their first glove and new bat. Let their approach be simple...See the ball; hit the ball. See the ball; catch the ball. See the mitt; pitch to it. Simplify the game for them today, and let them play for the love of the game." Amen and War Eagle

May 22, 2015 6:29am

Game Day Prayer

"Dear Lord,

Thank you for such a beautiful day. Help our players trust the wisdom of their coaches today. They have prepared them for today. Continue to simplify the game for them. See the ball; catch it. See the ball; hit it. See the mitt; pitch to it. May all that the players, coaches, fans, and parents do today bring honor to You." Amen and War Eagle

May 23, 2015 7:57am

Game Day Prayer

"Dear Lord,

Thank you for being the most patient Coach. You put our players in the same situation until they learned their lesson. Thank you for helping them transition yesterday from pressing the, 'We believe you, Coach, button,' to 'Hey, we can do this. Let's go.' Thank you for allowing me to see that transition. Continue to keep today a simple day. See the ball; catch it. See the ball; hit it. See the mitt; pitch to it. May all that the players, coaches, fans, and parents do today bring honor to You." Amen and War Eagle

May 24, 2015 7:59am

Prayer of Thanks

"Thank You, Lord, for the testimony we are witnessing through the Auburn Softball team. Thank you for having the final say." Amen and War Eagle

May 25, 2015 6:45am

Travel Day Prayer

"Dear Lord,

Thank you for such a beautiful travel day. Thank you for the send-off celebration that our players, coaches, fans, and parents will experience in a few hours. Please keep all traveling to OKC safe. Put angels in front of them, behind them, over them, beneath them, and beside them to keep them safe. May all who see them, talk to them, hear them, or think of them have You in their hearts." Amen and War Eagle

May 28, 2015 7:39am

Game Day Prayer

"Dear Lord,

Thank you for safe travels and for the wonderful journey You have brought to the Auburn Softball players, coaches, fans, and parents. Thank you for the testimony these young ladies and coaches are living. Help the entire softball family to be gracious, patient, and kind throughout this series. Please continue to keep our team's approach to the game simple. See the ball; catch it. See the ball; hit it. See the mitt; pitch to it. May all that our players, coaches, fans, and parents do bring honor to You and the

doubters asking themselves, 'what just happened?'
Thank you for having the final say." Amen and War
Eagle

May 30, 2015 8:15am

Game Day Prayer

"Dear Lord,

Thank you for the blessings You have showered on
the Auburn players, coaches, fans, and parents. You
have had this day planned since the beginning of time.
Every practice, hitting lesson, fielding lesson, camp,
and game our players have participated in and our
coaches have coached or given led to this moment.
Help our players and coaches bring those lessons
with them today. Give them courage and hope. Let
our players rise like a kite in the wind because a kite
only reaches its highest height against the opposing
wind. Let them soar to their highest heights today. Let
everything our players, coaches, fans, and parents
do today bring honor to You." Amen and War Eagle

May 31, 2015 9:12am

Game Day Prayer

"Thank you, Lord, for extending the Auburn University
softball season. When I prayed about what I would

post for today's prayer, the sentence, 'I am not finished,' came to mind. Thank you for not being finished in the lives of our players, coaches, fans, and parents. Today, help our players play with courage, confidence, and with the hope that the best softball is ahead. May all that the players, coaches, fans, and parents do bring honor to You." Amen and War Eagle

Jun 01, 2015 1:12am

Travel Day Prayer

"Dear Lord,

Please keep the players, coaches, fans, and parents safe as they travel back home today. May all who see them, talk to them, hear them, or think about them have You in their heart." Amen and War Eagle

Oct 11, 2015 7:25am

Game Day Prayer

"Thank you, Father, for Your blessings. Thank you for the Auburn softball coaches, coaches' families, players, parents, and fans. Today, help our players begin to see how all of the details fit into one master plan just like each of us fits into Your master plan. Help our players to see and understand their various roles today. Help all of us to be quick studies as You coach us to be like You. Help all of us to behave in such a way that others can see You in us and ask us what's different. Please keep both teams safe today as they play and as they travel." Amen and War Eagle

Oct 17, 2015 10:06am

Game Day Prayer

"Thank you, Father, for the blessings of today. Thank you for the chance to see old friends Coach Jimmy and Coach Belinda across the field. Thank you for the lessons You teach us on and off the field. Help our players, coaches, parents, and fans grow as a family throughout this season because there is no stronger tie than that of a family...those we are born into and those we choose to be a part of. Please keep both teams safe from injury, and give everyone safe travel home." Amen and War Eagle

Oct 24, 2015 7:08am

Game Day Prayer

"Dear Lord,

Please place Your angels around our players and those of the opposing team today and throughout this season to keep them safe from injury. Please keep them in the palm of Your hand. Thank you for Your promise that any weapon formed against one of Your children will not prosper. Please restore the health of those in our Auburn family. Thank you for the blessings of today and for the opportunity to watch our children. Thank you for the talents You have given the Auburn players and coaches. May all that the players, coaches, fans, and parents do bring honor to You." Amen and War Eagle

Jan 29, 2016 5:50am

"In everything give thanks, for this is the will of God in Christ Jesus concerning you." 1 Thessalonians 5:18

I can look back over my life and the lives of my daughters and see God's plan. The darkest "seasons" lead to the greatest rewards. I am not sure what everyone is facing. For me...trials come in seasons, not moments. I have faith that my current season will have rewards on the other side and that your will too. If God brought us to it, He will bring us through it.

Feb 10, 2016 4:58am

Travel Day Prayer

"Dear Lord,

Please protect the players, coaches, fans, and officials as they travel to Auburn. May anyone who sees them, talks to them, hears them, or thinks about them have You in their hearts." Amen

Feb 11, 2016 5:05am

Game Day Prayer

"Dear Lord,

Please keep Your hand of protection around both teams today. Keep them free from injury. Thank you for blessing each of these young ladies with a unique talent that completes our team. Help them to be One team, and help them to be students of the game, learning a little more with every pitch. Help our players, coaches, and fans to be good hosts and hostesses this weekend and for others to know by our actions that we serve You." Amen

Feb 12, 2016 5:37am

Game Day Prayer

"Dear Lord,

Thank you for the unique talent that You have given to each player and coach. Help them to recognize how special they are and the value they bring to the entire team. Help them to know each other's weaknesses and strengths so that they complete each other. Where one is weak, and one is strong; help them to complement each other. Help the players to accept the lessons You will teach them tonight, and help the players, coaches, and fans to bring honor to You with their actions." Amen

Feb 13, 2016 9:03am

Game Day Prayer

"Thank you, Lord, for the sunshine. Thank you for keeping all of the players injury free. Bind these 30 players and coaches in Love. Thank you for making them one unit. Thank you for the coaches and for the wisdom and discipline they are teaching our daughters. The greatest lesson they are learning is teamwork. That is a lesson they can take with them long after they graduate. I celebrate their lives, talents, and personalities. Thank you for the opportunity You have given me to get to know these amazing young ladies and their families. Bring them closer as one unit with every pitch." Amen

Feb 14, 2016 8:30am

Game Day Prayer

"Dear Lord,

Thank you for another beautiful day. Thank you for keeping all of the players safe. Thank you for building the confidence of our team with every pitch, every call, and every play. Help them to be students of the game, getting 1% better every time they practice or play. I ask Your hand of protection over the teams and fans as they return home today." Amen

Feb 16, 2016 4:48am

Travel Day Prayer

"Dear Lord,

Thank you for good travel weather. Thank you for Your continued hand of protection around the Auburn players, coaches, and staff. Please be with them today as they travel. Keep the bus driver alert. Put angels in front of them, beside them, above them, and underneath them. May anyone who sees them, hears them, talks to them, or thinks about them have You in his or her heart." Amen

Feb 17, 2016 5:30am

Game Day Prayer

"Dear Lord,

Thank you for the beautiful weather today. As our players line up today, help them to demonstrate through their words and actions that they serve You.

Set them apart so that others know something is different about them. Create a strong bond of love among them so that they are One team.

One pitch, One play, One team." Amen

Feb 18, 2016 5:07am

Travel Day Prayer

"Dear Lord,

Thank you for continuing to bless the Auburn softball players and coaches. Be with them today as they travel to Clearwater. Thank you for the leadership of the upperclassmen as they make sure everyone is in the right place at the right time with no Tiger left behind! Thank you for the folks behind the scenes running interference for our girls. It isn't easy planning for Auburn, party of 50 of more. Thank you for the people we don't see who are such a big part of this program. Set these young ladies apart so that others recognize there is something different about them, and the difference is You." Amen and War Eagle

Feb 19, 2016 8:23am

Game Day Prayer

"Dear Lord,

Thank you for a beautiful Florida day...it is a Floriday! Thank you for helping our players recognize and respect the officials-- what a lesson for all of us to see something differently than those with authority over us. Help them to adjust and to expand their definitions of the most basic elements of the game. This is a lesson that our daughters can take with them to the workplace. Help them to recognize the differences, adjust, and move forward. Thank you for setting our players and coaches apart, and help others to recognize there is something a little bit different about those Auburn Tigers. Please keep the players from all teams safe and injury free." Amen and War Eagle

Feb 20, 2016 9:08am

Game Day Prayer

"Dear Lord,

Thank you for another beautiful day. Thank you for the life lessons You are teaching through the daily interactions our daughters have with their teammates, coaches, officials, and players and coaches from other teams. Continue to keep players from all teams injury free. Help all of us to realize that we are a work in progress. Sometimes we will have setbacks. When the setbacks come, help us to realize You are working to make us stronger." Amen and War Eagle

Feb 21, 2016 7:31am

Game Day and Travel Day Prayer

"Dear Lord,

Thank you for the beautiful day. As our players toe up today, help them to remember the lessons that began the first day of practice. Give them the courage to trust what they have learned and to give their new skills a chance to develop. Give them the quiet confidence that they are right where they need to be. Continue to bind these young ladies and coaches together so that they can enjoy the benefits and joy of being on a team--One pitch, one play, one Team... ONE. Please give all teams and fans safe travels home. May anyone who sees them, talks to them, hears them, or thinks about them have You in his or her heart." Amen and War Eagle

Feb 22, 2016 6:10am

"Dear Lord,

Please give the Auburn Tigers returning to tests this morning and this week a clear mind and confidence." Amen

Feb 25, 2016 4:29am

Game Day Prayer

"Dear Lord,

Thank you for keeping the Auburn softball family safe through the storms Tuesday and Wednesday. Storms remind us of Your greatness. Thank you for the calm that comes after the storm. Thank you for the gift of Peace beyond understanding. Calm the minds of our players and coaches so that for 21 outs, they can have fun and fellowship together. Continue to bind them together so that they think and act as ONE. Please keep players from all teams injury free throughout this tournament." Amen

Feb 27, 2016 7:58am

Isaiah 40:31 "But those that wait upon the Lord shall renew their strength; they shall run and not be weary, and they shall walk and not faint."

Having two daughters in college who are also "A" students and Division 1 athletes, friends who work shift work, friends who have young children or aging parents, and friends who work more than one job, brings this promise [Isaiah 40:31] to mind, and I am claiming renewed strength for all of us. I see folks going on naps versus a night's sleep. God also never puts more on us than we can handle. He must have MUCH confidence in us. Today's challenge is to offer a hand to the college student, friend, parent, child, or spouse whose wagon is full. Be the blessing.

"Dear Lord,

Open our eyes so that we can be a blessing to others. Renew our strength so that we can finish the race strong." Amen

Feb 27, 2016 8:03am

Game Day Prayer

"Dear Lord,

Lift our players up on eagles' wings today. Renew their strength. Bring smiles to their faces, and help them to play for the love of the game. Continue to set them apart so that it is evident that they are different, and the difference is You." Amen

Feb 28, 2016 8:03am

Game Day Prayer

"Heavenly Father,

Continue to renew the strength of our players. Their days start early and end late. This is the part of softball that no one sees unless they have been part of a collegiate program. But You see their efforts and their hard work. Multiply their efforts, and bless their work. Give them opportunities to see the lessons they have learned in practice. Help them to teach each other and to be quick studies. Give the coaches an abundance of patience and love for these young ladies. These young ladies are like roses...the rose gardener knows that there are lots of thorns in the rose stems, but he grows roses anyway because they are so beautiful and fragrant. Help our coaches and our players to love each other---thorns and all so that we can grow those roses." Amen

Mar 04, 2016 6:27am

Isaiah 40:31

"But those who hope in the Lord will renew their strength. They will soar on wings like eagles; they will run and not grow weary; they will walk and not be faint."

This is a promise that I am claiming for my family and friends. Say the words aloud. I know my daughters go from early to late as do many college students and athletes. I know that my friends, family, and I work long hours. I have friends with young children, sickness, and aging parents that are working extra long hours because of the emotions connected.

My prayer

"Dear Lord,

Thank you for Your promises. Lift us up on eagles' wings. Thank you for hope and renewed strength. Thank you for the rain cancellations this week so that the Auburn softball family could renew their strength. Thank you for keeping us safe. Set us apart so that it is evident that You live in our hearts. Please keep all teams, families, and fans safe as they travel to Auburn this weekend." Amen

Mar 05, 2016 10:58am

Game Day Prayer

"Dear Lord,

May all we say and do today be said and done from the heart. Please keep all players safe. Thank you for the gift of today. We are exchanging a day of our life for today. Help all that we do be for Your honor and not our own." Amen

Mar 06, 2016 8:54am

What a great day to spend time with family and friends! Game day prayer.

"Dear Lord,

Thank you for answered and unanswered prayers. Help our Auburn family to recognize You are in control, and we can't see the whole picture. Bind the players and families together as one unit. Thank you for Your loving kindness and for Your discipline. Give our players an open mind and the courage to grow. Help each player to recognize her uniqueness and to have the courage to be herself. Help all of us to realize that when You made us, You said, 'Ta Dah.' Help us to live up to our potential so that we are worthy of Your 'Ta Dah.'"

Amen

Mar 09, 2016 5:29am

Game Day Prayer

"Dear Lord,

Thank you for equipping our daughters for the storms of life. Just as the coaches prepare them for games and facing pitchers, You prepare them for life. Thank you for holding their hands as they transition from teenagers to young adults. Thank you for the role models that surround them every day. Continue to set them apart so that others can see and will ask what's different about them...and the difference is You. Please keep all players, coaches, and fans safe today as they travel and play."

Amen

Mar 12, 2016 7:41am

Game Day Prayer

"Dear Lord,

Thank you for a beautiful day. Help the Auburn Tigers to play to the best of their abilities, and help the players to carry the skills they have learned in practice to the field. Please keep all players safe this weekend. Thank you for the opportunity You have given all of us to support our daughters today and always." Amen

Mar 14, 2016 5:34am

Game Day Prayer

"Dear Lord,

Thank you for keeping players from both teams safe and for grace the coaches and players have shown with those in authority over the game. At the end of the day, our players and coaches will be stronger for it. Thank you for the opportunity to play such a strong opponent early in the season. When we play strong opponents, we will get stronger. Our weaknesses will be exposed, and there is time to learn from and to grow from those exposures. Just like life, help our daughters to realize that it is not where we start that is important, it is where we finish." Amen

Mar 16, 2016 5:34am

Travel and Game Day Prayer

"Dear Lord,

Thank you for keeping our players, coaches, and fans in the palm of Your hand. Keep them safe as they travel to Birmingham and then on to Starkville. Please continue to keep a hedge of protection around them. May all who see them, talk to them, hear them, or think about them have You in their hearts. Continue to grow their knowledge and skills of the game so that each time they hit the field they get 1% better than they were the day before. Thank you for Your grace and patience." Amen

Mar 19, 2016 9:06am

Game Day Prayer

"Dear Lord,

Thank you for safe travels to Starkville, MS. Thank you for the opportunity to fellowship and to watch our daughters learn the principles of teamwork. Last night, we watched records being broken for both Auburn and Mississippi State. Help that experience teach our daughters that we set limits, but You do not. You provide limitless opportunities when we trust You. Continue to keep the players from both teams safe. Please give all of our players a cup of courage and quiet confidence as they step onto the field today. Help others to see You in all that the players, coaches, and fans do today." Amen

Mar 20, 2016 12:30am

Game Day Prayer

"Dear Lord,

Thank you for the hospitality that Starkville has shown the Auburn players and fans this weekend. Thank you for the lessons You continue to teach through softball. Help each player to recognize that You are a patient Teacher and that You will continue to place her in the same situation until she learns the lesson she is supposed to learn. Some lessons are harder to learn than others, but the little lessons must be learned first. Just like a runner has to go to first base before she goes to second base, the lessons You have for us to learn are sequential. Help our daughters to continue to band together and to grow as one unit. Help them to play to each other's strengths and to play to their full potential. Help others to see You in their actions. Help them to realize that they are right where they need to be."

Amen

Mar 23, 2016 6:38am

Game Day Prayer

"Dear Lord,

Thank you for Your continued blessings. Help our daughters realize that they are not defined by a number or by what others say or think about them. They are defined by You. Help them see themselves through Your eyes. Please keep them safe as they travel to and from Atlanta today." Amen

Mar 24, 2016 5:15am

Our Tigers had a rough start yesterday, and as the game progressed, the announcer kept bringing up the mistakes that were made early in the game. Granted, the mistakes were made...there's no denying that. It made me appreciate the incredible grace our daughters show on and off the field. It also made me remember that it is not the mistake, it is what we do after the mistake that defines us. I was also reminded that we are going to have people in our lives with long memories of our mistakes, but we serve a Savior who forgets our mistakes. He paid the price for them.

Hebrews 8:12

"For I will forgive their wickedness and will remember their sins no more."

Mar 25, 2016 1:04pm

Game Day Prayer

"Dear Lord,

On this Good Friday, let us remember the price You paid for loving us. Thank you for loving us. May all that we do honor You." Amen

Mar 26, 2016 9:28am

Game Day Prayer

"Dear Lord,

Thank you for paying for our sins in full. Thank you for the blessing of family and friends and for the opportunity to be with both this Easter weekend. Thank you for the blessing of athleticism that You gave our daughters and for the coaches and trainers You have placed in their lives. Continue to bind the players, coaches, and families together. Thank you for covering us in Your blood and for forgiveness." Amen

Mar 31, 2016 4:53am

Travel Day Prayer

"Dear Lord,

Send Your angels to provide invisible protection from danger of collision, storms, fire, explosions, bruises, and illness for the Auburn softball players, coaches, and fans today as they travel to Kentucky. Intervene on their behalf so that their travels are smooth. Keep the bus driver alert and cheerful. May all who see them, talk to them, hear them, or think about them have You in their hearts. May all that they do this weekend bring honor to You. Continue to set these young ladies and coaches apart, and bind them together in love." Amen

Apr 01, 2016 4:56am

Game Day Prayer

"Dear Lord,

Thank you for keeping the Auburn softball family safe while they traveled to Kentucky. Thank you for keeping Your angels encamped about them. What a comfort to those of us thousands of miles away to know that You have placed angels in charge of our daughters' safety. Continue to help the players learn more about each other so that they will play to each other's strengths. Bind them in love so that they will do anything for each other. Give them a quiet confidence to know they are right where they need to be. Let them see what You see when they look in the mirror: perfection. Set them apart so that it is evident they are special, and open doors for questions to be asked, and the answer will be You."

Amen

Apr 02, 2016 7:06am

Game Day Prayer

"Dear Lord,

Thank you for keeping Your promises. Thank you for Your protection, grace, and mercy. Thank you for setting this program apart. Help the players to continue to learn more about each other and to celebrate their differences because where one is weak, others are strong. Thank you for binding them together in love." Amen

Apr 02, 2016 7:16am

Hang in there...restoration is coming. God will pay you back 7 times for every item the devil has stolen from you. So for every tear, seven smiles...for every dollar, seven dollars, for every put down, seven atta girls, for every day of pain, seven days pain free...

For the athletes in my life....for the pitchers...for every walk, seven strike outs...For the hitters...for every strike out, seven hits. For the defensive players, for every bad throw or bobble, seven putouts. My point is the devil will focus on the misses and pain in our lives. God focuses on restoration, and we should too!

Apr 03, 2016 6:59am

Game Day Prayer

"Dear Lord,

Today, 2,016 years ago, You died on the cross for our sins. You conquered death, and Your blood covered our sins, the sins of our children, and the sins of our children's children. Thank you for the price You paid for us. You are a God of Hope and Victory. Help our players, coaches, support staff, fans, and parents take a moment today to remember You and the price that You paid for us because of Your love for us. Help our team to remember that the greatest gift we can ever have is love. In fact, You command us to love one another. Help our team to feel Your love and the love that we have for them as parents, coaches, team-mates, and fans. Love can conquer anything because there is nothing--even death--that we won't do for each other if we truly know the meaning of LOVE." Amen and War Eagle

Apr 03, 2016 6:59am

Game Day and Travel Day Prayer

"Dear Lord,

Thank you for loving our daughters and families. Thank you for shielding them from the darts the devil throws their way. Close their ears so that they only hear their coaches' and teammates' voices. Help their actions and words to reflect You. Please send Your angels to encamp about them today during the game and as they return home to Auburn. Please renew their strength and their spirits not only for the game, but for the week ahead. Set them apart so that others can 'see' there is something different about them. The difference is You, and may the difference provide opportunities for giving others hope and a chance to talk about Your amazing grace and love." Amen

Apr 06, 2016 5:21am

Happy Wednesday. We serve a God who heals. I believe God can work through doctors. Feeling blessed for the doctors who have helped my daughters and family through the years...including my dad, Thomas Merritt, and for the doctors to be... Kasey Cooper. Blessed that our doctor's bedside manner includes prayer.

Apr 06, 2016 6:04am

Game Day Prayer

"Dear Lord,

Thank you for the softball family and for the lifetime friends who have been brought into our lives through softball. Thank you for the moments on the softball field that turn into memories for smiles on another day. Thank you for giving our daughters the gift of athleticism. May all that they do on and off the field bring honor to You. Help them to play above their potential. Please keep both teams safe from injury." Amen

To quote Ms. Amy, "This is the last time Kasey Cooper and Kate Benton square up. They have played side by side and against each other for the past 13 years, and we loved every minute of it."

Apr 08, 2016 2:23pm

Game Day Prayer

"Dear Lord,

Thank you for the opportunity for our daughters and coaches to support the families who have been touched and are currently being touched by breast cancer. This weekend is about Hope! Please keep them safe, and help them bring awareness to the fight against breast cancer and support for the families touched by it." Amen

Apr 12, 2016 5:38am

The Lord came to restore and to heal us. He is the Master Physician.

Apr 13, 2016 2:53pm

Game Day Prayer

"Dear Lord,

Thank you for the blessings of today. Help our daughters to focus on the present because the present is Your gift to us. Please restore those who need restoration both mentally and physically. You know those needs. Thank you for setting these young ladies apart." Amen

Apr 15, 2016 5:48am

Happy Friday! Game Day Prayer

"Dear Lord,

Thank you for Your continued blessings of restoration and healing. I am claiming restoration over these young ladies. Give them clear minds, and still their restless hearts with the peace that only You can bring. Restore those that need Your touch. You know who they are. Thank you for setting these young ladies and coaches apart. You are able. Let them play for the love of the game, and let others see You in all that they do." Amen

Apr 16, 2016 7:54am

Game Day Prayer

"Dear Lord,

Thank you for Your promises of restoration. When You restore us, You give us back more than was taken. Thank you for this season of restoration. Thank you for restoring health, a clear mind, and a courageous spirit." Amen

Apr 17, 2016 6:23am

Game Day Prayer

"Dear Lord,

Thank you for the restoration season and for setting these young ladies and coaches apart." Amen

Apr 20, 2016 6:19am

Game Day Prayer

"Dear Lord,

Thank you for the coaches You have put over the Auburn softball players and staff. Each day, they learn lessons that they will carry with them long after they leave Auburn. Thank you for the lesson the Auburn players and coaches teach the fans and parents are learning.

hard work + perseverance + humbleness + love = one great team

May all that the players and coaches do bring honor to You."

Amen

Apr 22, 2016 5:59am

Game Day Prayer

"Dear Lord,

Thank you for loving our daughters and coaches. Thank you for walking ahead of them, preparing them, and for ensuring they will have everything they need--physically, mentally, and materialistically for the challenges they will face. Just as the tree was there when Zacchaeus needed it, I trust that You will provide for our daughters, coaches, and for us. Thank you for being our Provider. Help our daughters and us to recognize the 'trees' You have planted in our paths."

Amen

Apr 23, 2016 7:31am

Game Day Prayer

"Dear Lord,

Your strength is made perfect in our weakness. Help our daughters to see that they can do anything through You. Your grace is sufficient. Through all the excitement, provide opportunities for fans, other players, and friends to recognize there is something different about these young ladies and coaches...and the difference is You. Thank you for setting these young ladies apart. Continue to bind them in love." Amen

Apr 24, 2016 7:19am

Game Day Prayer

"Dear Lord,

Thank you for the blessings You have showered on the Auburn softball family-players, coaches, parents, and fans. Thank you for continuing to set these young ladies and coaches apart. Give all of us opportunities to talk about our journey to You. Thank you for being in charge and for going before us to plan our path. Help all of us to stay on Your path." Amen

Apr 29, 2016 5:40am

Travel Day Prayer

"Dear Lord,

Please cover the Auburn softball players, coaches, fans, and drivers with Your protection today as they travel to Tennessee. Please put Your angels over them, underneath them, beside them, in front of them, and behind them. May all who see them, talk to them, hear them, or think about them have You in their hearts."

Amen

Apr 30, 2016 5:37am

Game Day Prayer

"Dear Lord,

I want to praise You for bringing these young ladies and coaches together. Thank you for the talent each one brings to the team. Truly, they are complete as a team, just like we are complete in You. Thank you for continuing to restore these young ladies and coaches. Continue to send Your angels to keep charge over them. Thank you for setting them apart, and help others to continue to notice that there is something different about these young ladies and coaches, and the difference is You. May all that they do bring honor to You." Amen

May 01, 2016 6:20am

Game Day Prayer

"Dear Lord,

Thank you for giving a little common sense to the decision makers last night. The decision to postpone last night's game kept all of the players safe. Today, I ask You to renew our players' strength. Their coaches have prepared them all season to play three games in one day; today they play two. You are a God that gives us more than enough. Thank you for giving our daughters, 'More than enough strength' today. Thank you for this restoration season. May every hit that has been taken from our hitters be paid back seven times. May every strike that has been called a ball for our pitchers be paid back with seven strikes. May every doubt our players have had be paid back with a confident spirit. May others look at our players and shake their heads because they can't understand what sets these young ladies apart. That question will give all of us a chance to share the difference... You. You are the difference maker." Amen

May 02, 2016 5:26am

Game Day Prayer

"Dear Lord,

Thank you for being the potter in our lives. Help us to always yield to Your guidance and to Your hands. Help our players, coaches, parents, and fans be 'moldable' so that You can create a masterpiece. Thank you for taking 'people' pieces and molding them together to create a masterpiece. Give our team patience. I believe much joy and celebration is headed their way as long as they yield to Your hands. Continue to mold these young ladies and coaches so that they can be Your masterpiece. Thank you for not being finished yet...with all of us."

Amen

May 03, 2016 5:27am

Finals Prayer

"Dear Lord,

Thank you for safe travels home for our Auburn softball players, coaches, and fans. They have been gone since Friday, been on the softball field 15 hours, been in a bus 12 hours, and somewhere in between, they have studied for exams. Some will walk into exams today after getting in late last night, and others will have exams every day the remainder of the week. Please give them clear minds and peace as they sit down to take their finals and as they push to turn in final projects. More is expected of them, and I know You will give them the perseverance and stamina to finish the tasks in front of them. Thank you for setting them apart." Amen

May 04, 2016 5:21am

Happy Wednesday

I am sending prayers of perseverance for my college peeps and for my Farley family.

"Dear Lord,

Rain down confidence, peace of mind, a joyful spirit, and perseverance so that we can finish the race before us." Amen

May 06, 2016 5:08am

We made it.

"Dear Lord,

Thank you that the school season is over for our daughters and coaches. Thank you for giving all of them the strength to finish strong. As we celebrate our seniors this weekend, bring back to them memories of late nights, the tears, the challenges, the dropped classes, the project deadlines, the laughs, the intern jobs, the bus trips, the big plays, the celebrations, and the losses. Help them to draw upon all of these experiences because these are the experiences that helped our daughters grow and become who they are today. As they face the remainder of their season, help them to do so using all of the tools You have given them. The rest of the season is theirs, and it starts today. Give them the confidence to take it." Amen

May 07, 2016 7:24am

Game Day Prayer

"Dear Lord,

Thank you for always being there when we stumble. Help our daughters and us to reach out to grab Your hand. Thank you for the lessons You are teaching us. I am reminded of a little one learning to walk...

the baby never says, 'This walking thing just isn't for Me.' He continues to get up. Help us to keep getting up." Amen

May 08, 2016 8:24am

Game Day Prayer

"Dear Lord,

Give her the reward she has earned, and let her works bring her praises."

Amen

May 09, 2016 5:08am

Prayers for Kelsey Bogaards. She left it all on the field--months of rehab to get healthy to return to the dirt for her teammates. We should all live each day like it is the last day we have to do what we love. Prayers are going up.

May 09, 2016 11:55pm

"Thank you, Lord, for the physicians whose hands You guide. Thank you for healing our bodies. You are the Master Physician." Amen

May 11, 2016 6:25am

Happy Wednesday

"Thank you for loving us, Lord. Thank you for Your favor in my family's life and over the Auburn softball family. Thank you for continuing to set them apart." Amen

May 12, 2016 6:16am

Game Day Prayer

"Dear Lord,

Thank you for safe travels to Starkville. Thank you for the athletic talent You have given each player and for the wisdom of the coaches. Help them to learn from every pitch and to apply the lessons they have been learning this season and in seasons past in today's game. Thank you for Turtle's successful surgery and now recovery. Help our daughters to play each game as if it were their last and to leave all of their effort on the field. Help all of us to represent You in all that we do." Amen

May 13, 2016 5:44am

Happy Friday! I heard you all saw a beautiful rainbow yesterday. I love rainbows, and once, I saw and walked through the "end" of a rainbow. I will never forget it. Genesis 9:13

"I have placed my rainbow in the clouds. It is the sign of my covenant with you and with all the earth."

"Dear Lord,

Thank you for always keeping Your promises to us and for giving us a symbol of Your love and Your promise. Thank you for bringing Turtle to Starkville! What a blessing she is to this team. Help our daughters to leave it all on the field today and to play boldly. Help them to represent You in all that they do. Thank you for keeping them safe, and I ask You to keep all of the players free from injury. Heal those who have been injured." Amen

May 14, 2016 5:37am

Game Day Prayer

"Dear Lord,

Thank you for Your favor and for the lessons of faith and perseverance that You are teaching not only to our daughters, but also to anyone who follows the Auburn softball team. You know their hearts, and You know their future. Give them the courage to step out and to believe in themselves. They are right where they are supposed to be, and with Your spirit running through their bodies, they have everything they need to be successful. Filter what they hear so that they only hear their coaches and words of encouragement. Filter what they see so that they only see their coaches, teammates, and friendly faces. Help them to continue to play in such a way that others will shake their heads and say, 'What just happened?' Let them live their testimony." Amen

May 15, 2016 9:50am

Happy Sunday:)

"Dear Lord,

Thank you for setting the Auburn softball players and coaches apart. Thank you for giving all of us a chance to see that You have a purpose for everything that happens in our lives---especially when we can't see the purpose or understand the purpose. I know heads are shaking about what happened this weekend. Thank you for the head shaking, and thank you for bringing this group of young ladies together as One Team. I ask that You continue to keep a hedge of protection around these young ladies and coaches. Thank you for the chapter You are writing in their lives." Amen

May 18, 2016 5:01am

Happy Wednesday!

Isaiah 54:17 "No weapon formed against you shall prosper, and you will refute every tongue that shall rise against thee in judgement." God's got this.

May 20, 2016 5:28am

Game Day Prayer

"Dear Lord,

Thank you for Your blessings. You have blessed this program, these players, and the coaches so much, and I praise you for it. As our daughters and coaches approach this series, help them draw upon the lessons they have learned along the way. You have prepared them for anything they may see. Simplify the game for them, and help them play for the love of the game. Help them to get 1% better with every out. We are 210 outs from a national championship. Help these young ladies to play one out at a time... One pitch, one hit, one throw, one run, one team. ONE." Amen

May 21, 2016 8:39am

Happy Saturday and Gameday:)

"Dear Lord,

Thank you for the coaches You have put into these young ladies' lives. As I watch each player step into the batter's box, I look to third base, and Coach is smiling and saying, 'You can do this,' and I look to first base, and Scott is anxiously awaiting her arrival. I look to the dugout, and Corey is smiling and offering words of encouragement. When the pitchers are toeing up, every pitch is called from the dugout. In some cases, a timeout is called, and usually with an arm around the shoulders, a special dose of encouragement is given. 'You can do this.' Every player is placed on defense based on the hitter and the pitch call. Every step on defense, every swing, and every pitch our daughters make is guided. What a great lesson for all of us. What a great relationship we can have with You. You are right there to guide us, to offer words of encouragement, to discipline us, and to love us. Thank you for being our forever Coach. Thank you for loving us." Amen

May 22, 2016 10:31am

Game Day Prayer

"Dear Lord,

Thank you for the blessings You continue to rain down on our daughters and the Auburn softball program. I know that the best is yet to come. Thank you for the testimony that is being lived today." Amen

May 28, 2016 9:03am

Game Day Prayer

"Dear Lord,

Thank you for the blessings You continue to shower down on the Auburn softball program. As these young ladies face today, continue to give them a quiet confidence that only You can give. Simplify the game for game for them. Help them play with the joy they had growing up, and help them reap the rewards of their hard work." Amen

May 29, 2016 7:43am

Game Day Prayer

"Dear Lord,

Thank you for the blessings of today and for Your love. As our daughters go into today's games, help them to do so with confidence and peace of mind. Help them to see themselves as You see them versus seeing themselves as a series of statistics. Thank you for letting us hit the reset button every Morning---in fact every minute---and for keeping our statistics on a score board. Thank you for being right beside our daughters everywhere they go. Give them courage today and a spirit of boldness. May all that they do bring honor and glory to You." Amen

May 30, 2016 6:06am

Travel Day Prayer

"Dear Lord,

As teams, fans, and family members from across the country board planes and busses and cars in caravans begin their journey to OKC today, I ask You to run interference for them. Put a hedge of protection around them. May all who see them, hear them, talk about them, talk to them, or think about them have You in their hearts. May all that they do bring honor and glory to You." Amen

Jun 02, 2016 12:56am

Game Day Prayer

"Dear Lord,

Thank you for the blessings You continue to shower down on the Auburn softball players and coaches. What a joy it is for these young ladies to play in the Women's College World Series. Continue to give them a quiet confidence and peace of mind as they step onto the field today. Help them to play to their potential, and help them get stronger with each hour. Thank you for uniting this team and allowing them to experience what it means to play as ONE." Amen

Jun 04, 2016 8:01am

Game Day Prayer

"Dear Lord,

Thank you for the Auburn softball family and fans. What a blessing it is to be around so many people who love our daughters. As our daughters and coaches go into today, continue to fill them with a quiet confidence and humble spirit. Help them to know they are right where they are supposed to be. You have put the coaches and experiences in their lives to prepare them for any situation they may see. Thank you for helping them work together as ONE team towards ONE goal...one out at a time." Amen

Jun 05, 2016 9:16am

Game Day Prayer

"Dear Lord,

Thank you for the courage our daughters displayed on the field yesterday. They fought as one team just like You fight to bring the story of salvation to the lost. Thank you for using this program to teach our daughters what it means to be a part of something bigger than they are. Thank you for using softball to teach them about sacrifice, discipline, courage, trust, and love. As they go into today's game help them to trust their coaches, teammates, themselves, and most of all, You. You have ensured they have had experiences and people throughout their lives to prepare them for today. This team is not here by accident; they are here because of You. Continue to give them a peace that passes all understanding and a quiet confidence." Amen

Jun 06, 2016 9:19am

Game Day Prayer

"Dear Lord,

Thank you for the opportunity You gave our daughters today to use the gifts You gave them to play a sport they love. Please grant them the courage and strength to play with a warrior's heart, to be champions in Your eyes, and to finish what You started---so that when this day is over they can know in their hearts they did their best, and they can turn their eyes to You." Amen

Jun 07, 2016 8:50am

Happy Tuesday! Game Day Prayer

"Dear Lord,

Thank you for the gift of a new day. Thank you for the athletic gifts You have given our daughters. As they go into tonight's game, help them to do so with confidence and courage. Help them to play to their potential and to continue to play as ONE team with one heartbeat. Thank you for the testimony they are living and the thousands of lives they have touched this week. May all that they do bring honor to You." Amen

Jun 08, 2016 8:54am

Game Day Prayer

"Dear Lord,

Thank you for 'Three more Days' and the many other blessings You continue to shower down on our daughters and the coaches of the Auburn softball team. Help them to continue to play with a warrior's heart and to go into tonight's game with confidence, peace of mind, and calmness. Help them to gain confidence with each pitch and to play to the potential of the athletic gifts that You gave them. Continue to help them to communicate, to lift each other up, and to keep moving forward tonight. Help them to leave it all on the field, and I ask You to give them the benefits of their labor. Thank you for allowing them to live their testimony in front of thousands, so that they can turn others to You because of this experience." Amen

Jun 11, 2016 11:36pm

Travel Day Prayer

"Dear Lord,

Please keep the Team USA players, coaches, and staff safe as they travel from across this nation to OKC. Many of the players will be traveling alone, and I ask that You protect them, and show all of them favor as they make their way. May all who see them, talk to them, hear them, or think about them have You in their hearts. May all that they do bring honor to this country and to You. Bless them, and keep them safe until they return home to their families."

Amen

Jun 16, 2016 5:11am

Game Day Prayer

"Dear Lord,

Today, the Team USA players and coaches play their first 2016 game. They represent everything that is good about this country. I ask that You send Your angels to keep charge over them today and throughout this season. Help them to live up to the words on one of Olympic shirts, 'We can. We will. We are. One nation. One team.' May all that they do bring honor to You. We are one nation, under God." Amen

Jun 20, 2016 5:05am

Travel Day Prayer

"Dear Lord,

Thank you for the opportunity You have given Kasey, her teammates, and her coaches to travel to Japan. It is going to be a long day for them. Run interference for them, Lord. Show them favor and grace. Give them an abundance of energy and patience as they make their journey. Give them opportunities to share Your love throughout this trip. May they be met with smiles and kindness for the duration of this trip. Give Your angels charge over them to keep them safe. May all who see them, talk to them, hear them, or think about them have You in their hearts." Amen

Jun 23, 2016 4:21am

Game Day Prayer

"Dear Lord,

Thank you keeping our players and coaches safe. Today, they are playing in front of 20,000 fans that are most likely Not cheering for them. Help them to only hear the voices of their coaches and team mates. Use this experience to bind them together as one team. Help them to play to their strengths and to get better with every pitch. May all that they do bring honor to You." Amen

Jun 24, 2016 7:28pm

Last day in Japan for Team USA Softball.

"Dear Lord,

Thank you for keeping Your hand of protection around these young ladies and coaches. As they prepare for their last game, help them to do so with the confidence that they are right where they need to be. Reward them for their hard work, and help them continue to be ambassadors for You and for our country. May they continue to bond as one unit---with each one serving in a unique role. Help them to see themselves as You see them—beautifully and wonderfully made." Amen

Jun 25, 2016 6:44am

And so Team USA finished on a win:) I am so proud of them. They are getting better with every pitch, and there are many days of softball ahead of them. The best is yet to come.

"Dear Lord,

Thank you for the blessings You have given to these young ladies and coaches. They are touching people that they will never meet in person. Please bring them home to their families so that they can recharge and prepare for the remainder of their season. Continue to bind these young ladies and coaches together. They are on a steep learning curve. Thank you for the personal and team challenges You are putting in their paths. Overcoming these challenges is preparing them for the battles that lie ahead. You give Your toughest battles to Your strongest warriors." Amen

Jul 08, 2016 7:58am

Happy Friday!

"Dear Lord,

Continue to bind the Team USA players and coaches together. Help them to use the athletic and leadership gifts You have given to each one to give hope to the little girls across this nation who want to grow up to be just like them. Thank you for using them as a beacon of hope! Please give Your angels charge over their safety. Thank you for bringing them together as One Team. You teach us that a cord of 3 is not easily broken. Help them be a cord of 23."

Amen

Jul 09, 2016 9:13am

"Dear Lord,

Thank you for my amazing daughters and husband. Thank you for allowing me to be in the presence of so many wonderful young ladies, coaches, and families this week. Please continue to keep Your wings of protection around them as they represent everything that is great about our country. Keep the chaos away from them. Help them to continue to grow in their knowledge of the game, in their skills, and in their love for each other." Amen

Jul 10, 2016 12:20am

Go Team USA. 42 outs away from Gold!

"Dear Lord,

As these young ladies go into today's games, give them the quiet confidence that only You can give them. Give them the fruits of their labor, and help them to gain in their knowledge and skills with every pitch. Thank you for the hope that they give to all of the younger players who watch everything they do because they want to be just like them when they grow up. Thank you for the testimony they are living. The time will come when they will be asked, 'Did you ever...' And oh the stories they will be able to tell. Continue to keep them safe, and I ask that you heal those who have been injured. You know who they are." Amen

Jul 22, 2016 6:42pm

Happy Friday!

Team USA begins medal play tonight.

"Dear Lord,

Thank you for giving Your angels charge over the participating teams and coaches. Thank you for the friendships formed throughout this week and for allowing softball to be a platform for uniting people from around the world. Continue to bless the players, and give them the tenacity and renewed strength to finish strong." Amen

Jul 23, 2016 12:43pm

Happy Saturday!

Medal rounds continue today. Team USA plays Team Japan.

"Dear Lord,

Thank you for keeping the teams safe throughout this tournament. Thank you for the friendships that grow stronger and for those that are yet to be formed through this great sport. Thank you for the hope that all of the players are giving to the millions of little girls who look up to them. As Team USA goes into tonight's game against Japan, let them grow stronger with each pitch, and help them to draw upon the lessons and skills they have learned throughout this season. Help them to play to their strengths and to play with one heartbeat." Amen

Jul 24, 2016 11:50am

Happy Sunday!

I have been so blessed to watch Team USA this summer. All of the players seek excellence, and yesterday was no exception. They are getting better with every pitch, and through every missed opportunity, they are getting stronger.

Jul 27, 2016 9:10pm

"Dear Lord,

Thank you for continuing to keep the players, coaches, and fans from all teams safe throughout this week. Thank you for the life lessons You are teaching our daughters. Give them a quiet confidence as they step onto the field tonight. You have put coaches in their lives to prepare them, teammates in their lives to push them, and family in their lives to love them. Continue to help them play as One Team with One Heartbeat. May all that they do bring honor to You." Amen

Seeing young women with smiles on their faces after traveling thousands of miles and knowing they continued to smile after sleeping on cots in gyms reminded me and many other softball fans of how blessed I am. Some of the players that I know personally shared with me their main concern of having food when they returned to their native countries and how thankful they were that sister countries recently implemented open border policies so that they could cross over for food and other basic necessities like soap and toothpaste. So....if you have a roof over your head, food in the fridge, toothpaste, and soap....you are more blessed than many of the players from the 31 visiting countries that participated in the softball World Championship last week.

Oct 15, 2016 6:51am

Game Day Prayer

"Dear Lord,

Thank you for the blessings You have showered down on the Auburn softball players and coaches. As the players put on the Auburn jerseys for the first time this season, fill their hearts with excitement and joy and the confidence that they will see their hard work rewarded. I thank you for giving Your angels charge over them today. Please keep all players safe, and use this day to teach them lessons that they can carry with them throughout this season and their lives."

Oct 16, 2016 8:44am

Game Day Prayer

"Dear Lord,

Thank you for the Auburn softball players and coaches. As they approach this day, help our players believe in themselves and their coaches. They are learning to apply new skills, break bad habits, and bond with new teammates. Give them a desire to learn and the courage to take that first step. Help them to get 1% better every day...after all the difference between 211° and 212° is water boils at 212°. Give them patience as they begin to apply what they have learned." Amen

Oct 21, 2016 6:27am

Game Day Prayer

"Father,

As the players from both teams line up today, give them the courage to apply the skills they have learned in practice in the game. Courage is required to leave the familiar for the unfamiliar. Help our players trust their coaches and step out on faith. It takes 21 times in a row applying a new skill before our muscles commit the skill to memory. One miss, and we start over. Help us to count to 21 today. May all that our players, coaches, and fans do today bring honor to You." Amen

Oct 24, 2016 4:51pm

Congratulations Kasey Cooper! We are so proud of you:) what an honor for these 43 young ladies to be invited and to have the chance to wear USA across their chests.

Oct 29, 2016 5:19am

Game Day Prayer

"Dear Lord,

Thank you for teaching us that 'Two are better than one. If one falls the other can lift him up.' How much greater with an entire team. Teach our daughters to be encouragers of each other and to recognize when they need to lift each other up--both on and off the softball field. Thank you for being the Master Coach and Teacher in our lives and in the lives of our daughters. Lifting someone up is a skill, and skills have to be practiced to be perfected. I pray for Your grace, and I ask You to give our daughters opportunities to practice lifting each other up. Thank you for keeping Your hand of protection around the players and coaches from all teams today. Thank you for loving us before we loved You. Use us to bless others." Amen

Dec 31, 2016 5:05pm

Prayers for safe travels for all of these athletes and coaches as they travel to Clearwater, Florida for the opportunity to represent the USA while playing a sport they love. What a blessing:) U S A! U S A! U S A!

Jan 01, 2017 9:38am

A Prayer for 2017

"Dear Lord,

As I start 2017, let me be a blessing to others. Where there is impatience, let me be an example of patience. Where there is strife, let me be a peacemaker. Where there is hopelessness, give me the words to offer hope. Where there are unloved, let me love. Where there is injustice, give me the courage to speak up. Most of all help me to love others as You have loved me."

Amen

Feb 08, 2017 2:54am

Travel Day Prayer

"Father,

Please cover the players, coaches, and fans with Your hand of protection as they make their way to Puerto Vallarta today. Help them to be greeted with warm smiles everywhere they go. May all who see them, hear them, talk to them, or think about them have You in their hearts." Amen

Feb 10, 2017 10:38am

Game Day Prayer

"Dear Lord,

Thank you for the experience You are giving the AU players, coaches, and fans to play and watch the game we love in Puerto Vallarta. Help us to be ambassadors of You while we are here. Expose our weaknesses so that we can grow. Help our players and coaches to learn with every pitch so that they can fulfill the plans You have made for them. Help them to get 1% better every practice and every game, and help them to be eager for Your lessons." Amen

Feb 11, 2017 8:00am

Game Day Prayer

"Dear Lord,

Thank you for Your blessings. You have surrounded our daughters with coaches who know the game, trainers and doctors who keep them game ready, media specialists who snap great pictures, student coaches who are quick to bring a smile, and an athletic director who is willing to travel with the team. Our daughters are in good hands. These are the men and women that You have placed around them to teach them softball and to help them mature into strong young ladies who will make this world a better place. Help our daughters to trust what they have learned and to bring their best today and always. May others see Your grace and mercy in all that we do." Amen

Feb 12, 2017 7:53am

Travel Day Prayer

"Dear Lord,

As the players, coaches, support staff, fans, and parents head back to Auburn and many other cities across the USA, keep them safe. Send Your angels to keep charge over them. Put angels beside, beneath, above, below, ahead, and behind them to protect them. May all who see them, hear them, talk to them, or think about them have You in their hearts." Amen

Feb 16, 2017 5:28am

Game Day Prayer

"Dear Lord,

Thank you for today and the chance to see the AU softball team play on the Plains. Help the confidence of the players to grow with every pitch. Help them to become knitted together as one heartbeat. Help them to anticipate each other's actions and to respond accordingly. Help them to pick each other up and to continue to grow as ONE unit. One pitch. One play. One hit. One team. ONE!"

Amen

Feb 17, 2017 7:20am

Good Morning,

I'm sharing a softball story today. As I reflect on some of my most memorable softball moments, I think back to the days when I was a travel coach. Most of you know that I coached some that were called "uncoachable," and I loved them, and they trusted me...and we learned much together. We were not always in the championship games early in our time together and during those "learning" times, a former all american shared her story with my team. She played at a D1 school and was the catcher. She was also the #2 batter, and in a previous season, she was 0-42 in that spot. It was to the point that she asked her coach, "Are you sure you want me in the #2 spot? Don't you think you should move me down in the lineup, or let a designated hitter hit for me? Her coach told her, "You don't see what I see. You are my #2 hitter, and you will be an all-American. I'm leaving you in the #2 position." The season went on, and she did become an all-American, and she finished with an above 300 batting average. What a blessing that her coach believed in her more than she believed in herself. Sometimes we have to believe in others before they believe in themselves. As I sat at Jane B. Moore Field last night and the video ended with the word, "Believe," I smiled. Believe...what a great word. Be blessed today, and remember that you never know what it might mean to someone else when they know that you believe in them. Be blessed.

Feb 18, 2017 9:32am

Game Day Prayer

"Dear Lord,

Thank you for the successes and challenges that our daughters are experiencing. Continue to use the game of softball to show Your love and grace. Bind them together in love, and help them to continue to lift each other up. Give them the quiet confidence that only You can give them, and perfect them in their weakness as only You can do. Block out any negativity from their ears and minds, and help them feel Your love as they step out onto the field today." Amen

Feb 19, 2017 7:48am

Game Day Prayer

"Dear Lord,

Thank you for using the game of softball to shape our daughters. Often they see the coal; You see the diamond. Help them to recognize the tests and situations they are in are but for a season, and seasons past. Lessons build upon each other, and each test prepares them for the next battle. Thank you for preparing them for the battles they will face- both on and off the softball field. May they feel Your presence, and give them the confidence that they are equipped for battle before them." Amen

Feb 23, 2017 3:09pm

Game Day Prayer

"Dear Lord,

Thank you for today and for Your blessings. Thank you for the struggles and successes You give them. The successes build confidence, and the struggles force them to rely on each other. Continue to bind them together in love. Twenty-six are better than one because if one falls the other can pick her up. Help Auburn, party of 26 grow into Auburn, party of 1." Amen

Feb 24, 2017 12:07am

Game Day Prayer

"Dear Lord,

Thank you for Your continued favor on the Auburn Softball team. Thank you for the love that the Auburn community shows them. Help them continue to prosper and to grow as one unit. What a joy it is to watch the smiles on their faces when they are on the field and to watch them as they congratulate each other on a job well done or to offer encouragement when the outcome isn't what they want. Please give them the fruits of their labor. Help their hard work come to fruition. Give Your angels charge over all of them so that no injuries occur. May all that we do bring honor and glory to You." Amen

Feb 25, 2017 11:34am

Game Day Prayer

"Dear Lord,

Thank you for the beautiful day! Thank you for the opportunity to be with our daughters and to watch them grow into the players and young ladies You would have them to be. Thank you for the assurance that Your will Will prevail in their lives no matter what. Use softball to draw them closer to You. Thank you for keeping them safe. Continue to set them apart. They are the head and not the tail. Help Your presence in their lives to be so strong that others will know there is something different about them, and that difference is You. May all that they do bring honor and glory to You, and give them the chance to use their experiences as a witness for You." Amen

Mar 02, 2017 5:07am

Game Day Prayer

"Dear Lord,

Please give safe travels to the teams, fans, and parents that are coming to Auburn today. May they be greeted with warm smiles and Southern hospitality. Help us to be gracious hosts and hostesses while they are in town. Thank you for giving me the chance to see the players and parents continue to grow as one unit---loving each other, helping each other, covering each other in prayer. Thank you for the storms You send. Storms give You a chance to calm us and our children. Storms remind us that we might not be as strong as we think we are and that You are the Calmer of the winds and rain. You are the only one that can turn the storms of our lives into turning points. Thank you for loving our daughters. Continue to use them and their talents to bring others to You. Set them apart so that others begin to ask what's different about this program. All roads lead to You." Amen

Mar 03, 2017 8:17am

Game Day Prayer

"Dear Lord,

Thank you for the display of love I witnessed at Jane B. Moore field last night among the players, coaches, and fans. Your spirit was there. You promise us that wherever two or more are gathered in Your name, that You will be there. Throughout this weekend and this season, be with us. Continue to bring us to You. Thank you for using our daughters as a testimony to You. Thank you for the lesson the Liberty and AU softball players taught us last night as they prayed at the plate. Thank you for setting these young ladies apart. Bless the Liberty softball players and coaches. Thank you for using them to bless others. Use our daughters as a blessing to others. Bless them so that they may bless others. Thank you for the reminder that You are with us always--even at Jane B. Moore softball field." Amen

Mar 04, 2017 7:16am

Game Day Prayer

"Dear Lord,

Thank you for such a beautiful day in Auburn. Thank you for the opportunities You place in our lives and in the lives of our daughters. Open our eyes so that we may see." Amen

Mar 05, 2017 9:02am

Game Day Prayer

"Dear Lord,

Thank you for giving our daughters grace. I can't imagine seeing everything I do at work put up on a giant scoreboard...and media waiting relentlessly to ask questions, and fans waiting to get out on the field for a hug or autograph or both. As our daughters line up to play today, help them to realize they are more than a number. They are precious in Your sight, and there is nothing You won't do for them. Continue to lift them up, and draw them to You. Help them to realize they are princesses of a mighty kingdom, and You see them as princesses, for they are Your children, the children of a King. Give them the confidence to conquer whatever steps in their paths." Amen

Mar 08, 2017 4:57pm

Game Day Prayer

"Dear Lord,

Thank you for the poise, grace, and patience You are giving our daughters---Poise to face and learn from their Mistakes---Grace to smile through it all--- And patience to trust the process they are learning to master. May all that they do bring honor to You." Amen

Mar 10, 2017 4:42am

Game Day Prayer

"Dear Lord,

Thank you for the blessings You continue to shower down on the AU softball players and coaches. As they go into this opening SEC series, help them to do so fearlessly. Fear does not come from You. In fact You tell us over and over again, 'Fear not.' Give our daughters courage, a spirit of power, and discipline throughout this series. Help them to draw upon the lessons they have learned so far this year to conquer any challenges that come their way throughout the weekend. Please keep players and fans from both teams safe this weekend. Set these young ladies apart so that others recognize something is amazingly different about them, and that difference is You." Amen

Mar 11, 2017 6:21am

Game Day Prayer

"Dear Lord,

Thank you for giving our daughters the fruits of their labor. Thank you for the character they are gaining with each pitch that is thrown. Thank you for the joy and the tears that come from the ups and downs of the game. Thank you for the swings and misses---the strikes and missed pitches. Our daughters are learning that failure is part of the process, and in life, just like a softball game, there's another batter or pitch coming, and they are going to have to get back in the game. I saw that last night with our daughters. Thank you for bringing these young ladies together as one unit. You are teaching them how to work for a common goal and how to lift each other up. Each player has a job to do whether that job is a special one--like being a pinch hitter or figuring out the pitch calls from the opposing team, or a regular in the starting lineup, and it takes all of them to be successful. Thank you for the support staff, the student and graduate assistants who are in the background cheering, comforting, encouraging, or giving a loving kick in the rear to our daughters. Their love of these young ladies is amazing. Continue to keep them safe, and help them get 1% better and 1% more confident every time they step onto a softball field. Use softball as a platform for them to share their testimony and to mold them into the young ladies You want them to be." Amen

Mar 12, 2017 8:55am

Game Day Prayer

"Dear Lord,

Help our daughters put their trust in You. Today as they step onto Jane B. Moore field, help them to focus on the hope and confidence You have placed inside their hearts. Help them draw upon the courage and strength You have given them...they need only ask. Give each of them the revelation that You will help them and that You are with them everywhere they go including Jane B. Moore field." Amen

Mar 17, 2017 9:50am

Game Day Prayer

"Dear Lord,

Thank you for the testimony these young ladies are living on the big stage of softball. Every step they take is up for discussion and critique. Thank you for helping the players leave it all on the field and for giving them the courage to continue to put on their uniforms, tie up their shoelaces, and line up and play. At the end of the day, You know their hearts. You know their desires, and You have their past, present, and future. You are the only critic that matters. Reward them for their hard work. Close their ears to any negative words. Close their minds to any doubt. May all that they do leave the critics wondering how what they watched just happened. All roads lead to You." Amen

Mar 18, 2017 8:14am

When I'm sitting in a car or in this case...a very large truck---traveling hundreds of miles to watch AU softball, I pass some of the time thinking about what's going on in my life...Lots of change for me and my family has either just happened or is about to happen. I also tend to compare most everything in my life to some aspect of softball...sorry...I've been around the game as long as I can remember. This brings me to my epiphany...no matter what is going on in our lives, we can either be acted upon or we can act upon the situation. I for one, want to be the one acting upon---and I want my family to act upon and not be the ones being acted upon. I'm not going to leave my life, my decisions, to the whims or in some cases bad decisions of others. In softball, I've learned through 45 years of either playing or coaching, that we can't trust the officials. So...the life lesson for today to the softball players young and old is to take control, and take the officials out of your game plan. To my friends making life decisions...do whatever you have to do to take clear control over your game plan...it's too important to leave to the whims of others.

Mar 18, 2017 8:24am

Game Day Prayer

"Dear Lord,

Thank you for the beautiful weather in Tampa, Florida:) thank you for the safe travels of the fans and players. Thank you for the fellowship and friendships formed around softball and for the life lessons You teach on the field. As our daughters line up to play today, continue to set them apart. Continue to bring positive thoughts into their minds, and only allow them to hear encouraging words. Help them to lift up their teammates. Help them to play with determination and confidence. Please give them the fruits of their labor. You know their hearts. You see their work ethic. As they line up to play today, give them the quiet confidence that only You can give them. Slow down the game for them so that it really is as easy as counting to 3...One, Two, Three outs... One, Two, Three, throw my favorite pitch...One, Two, Three, I'm going to hit whatever pitch you throw... One, Two, Three, hit it to me..." Amen

Mar 19, 2017 6:44am

Game Day Prayer

"Dear Lord,

Thank you for Your continued grace and mercy. Thank you for keeping our daughters safe and for the reminder that YOU do not set limits. We set limits. Help our daughters continue to seek You and to use softball as a platform to bring others to You. You make the impossible possible and achievable. Continue to set these young ladies apart so that others will recognize there is something different about them... You." Amen

Mar 24, 2017 6:26am

Travel Day Prayer

"Dear Lord,

Be with the AU players, coaches, and support staff as they make their way to Gainesville, Florida. Thank you for the beautiful Florida sunshine that is waiting on them. As they make their way down the interstate, give Your angels charge over them. Bless the parents of both teams as they, too, travel to watch their daughters. In Jesus' name, I bind all unkind words from coming out of anyone's mouth that is in the presence of the players from both teams. May all that they hear be positive and uplifting. Thank you for Your blessings and for giving these young ladies softball as a platform to honor and glorify You." Amen

Mar 25, 2017 5:20am

Game Day Prayer

"Dear Lord,

Thank you for the opportunities You have given our daughters to put on a D1 softball uniform to represent their school, families, and You. As they go into today's game, help them to draw upon the skills they have honed and to apply those skills and lessons at the right time. Thank you for the coaches You have put in their lives to teach them about the game, but also about life and the skills required to be successful long after they take off their cleats for the last time. Continue to bind them together in love and to see each other through Your eyes---not what is, but what can be. Help the players from both teams to focus on what's going on inside the fence and on being the best that they can be. May all that they hear be positive and encouraging. May all that they do be a testimony to You." Amen

Mar 26, 2017 7:39am

Today is a new day.

"Dear Lord,

Thank you for renewing the strength of those who trust in You. Moments make us into the people You would have us to be, and they are like pieces of sand on a beach---they are nothing as pieces, but they are beautiful when they are combined into a beach. Give us the wisdom to understand that a moment is a little piece of sand on a beach and that You will use that moment to create a beautiful landscape…us." Amen

Mar 26, 2017 6:00pm

"Dear Lord,

When I step onto the field, help me to apply the skills, knowledge and talent You have given me. Give me clear mind and a confident spirit. Help me to foul off curve balls the officials and pitchers send my way. Keep me safe. Give me a warrior's spirit to battle until the last out. May all that I do honor You." Amen

Mar 27, 2017 6:09am

Game Day Prayer

"Dear Lord,

Thank you for the sharpening that is going on in Gainesville, Florida. May both teams sharpen one another and exploit weaknesses so that growth can occur. I praise You for using softball to teach lessons that can be used not only on the field but in life. Steel sharpens steel. Let the sparks fly so that our daughters can be the young ladies You would have them to be." Amen

Mar 31, 2017 5:25am

"Dear Lord,

Thank you for using all things to work for your glory. Thank you for preparing the AU players, coaches, and staff for this moment. Bind them in love, and cover them with Your protective hand. Help them to draw on Your Holy Spirit for strength and to fight with the heart of a warrior. Bring them peace of mind that only You can bring." Amen

Apr 01, 2017 10:17am

Game Day Prayer

"Dear Lord,

Thank you, Father, for leaning down to hear our prayers. Thank you for Your healing grace and mercy. Thank you for using softball to teach lessons that our daughters can use in their lives and not just on the field. Thank you for the outpouring of love our daughters have been shown and for the heartfelt prayers that are being prayed to lift them up. Bind them together in LOVE because LOVE always wins." Amen

Apr 02, 2017 8:43am

Game Day Prayer

"Dear Lord,

Thank you for the success the AU Tigers have experienced this weekend. Be with each player and coach today as they go into the final game against Georgia. Help them to realize that all of them are what makes AU softball successful and that as a band of sisters, they are unstoppable. Open their ears and thoughts to only positive thoughts and images. In Your name, I bind any negative thoughts or words from entering their minds or ears. I thank you for being with each player as they face battles that are only known to You, and I praise You for giving them the courage to fight and overcome any battle they are facing. I know that You give Your toughest battles to Your toughest warriors. Help them rise to the occasion and overcome." Amen

Apr 07, 2017 5:45am

Game Day Prayer

"Dear Lord,

Be with the coaches, staff, and players as they prepare for today's game. Continue to bind them together in LOVE, and cover them with Your mercy and grace. I thank you that Your plan for this season and for their lives is YOUR plan, and nothing can stop Your plans for this season or for their lives. Continue to use softball as a platform for these young ladies to witness for You and to live their testimony. Thank you for preparing them for the future. Allow them to reap the benefits of their hard work." Amen

Apr 08, 2017 8:52am

Game Day Prayer

"Dear Lord,

Thank you for allowing the AU players, coaches, and staff to learn Your principles. Alone, they will never be able to accomplish what they can accomplish together. Thank you for allowing me to witness them picking each other up when one is knocked down. They are learning to lean on each other, and as a band of sisters; they will not easily be broken. Continue to use softball to give them a platform to bring others to You. Every little challenge they face as individuals and as a team is an opportunity to band together to overcome and to become stronger. Thank you for the testimony they are living...one day all of them will be able to say at just the right time, 'Let me tell you a little story.' I praise You for giving them the fruits of their labor. You see the bruises. You see the hours they put in on their own. You see their hearts. Multiply their hard work exponentially so that to the outsider looking in, there is 'No way.' But there is a way...You are the way. You are in the restoration business, and I praise You for it." Amen

Apr 09, 2017 7:16am

Game Day Prayer

"Dear Lord,

Thank you for teaching our daughters about teamwork. To be on a team, one has to recognize the DIVERSITY of the team---with a range of abilities and gifts varying in function and in strength with every single one a vital and needed part of the team.

They are learning the MUTUALITY of being on a team---each member is dependent upon all of the other members of the team---no player is an island. Today, help them celebrate and value their diversity. Continue to bless them and to give them the fruits of their labor. May all that they do bring honor to You." Amen

Apr 12, 2017 6:05am

Game Day Prayer

"Dear Lord,

Thank you for continuing to set the AU softball players, coaches, and staff apart. Thank you for the lessons You are teaching through softball. Thank you for binding these young ladies together in love and for keeping them in the palm of your hand. Fill them with the quiet confidence that only You can bring. Filter the noise, and close their minds and ears to only positive thoughts and words of encouragement. You are in the restoration business, and I'm claiming restoration over these young ladies. May the struggles each has faced and the struggles that lie ahead make them stronger and leave the naysayers scratching their heads. You are a God of the future, and nothing can stop the plan You have for these young ladies or the AU softball program. Give these young ladies the fruits of their labor, and help others to ask questions about their success. All answers include You." Amen

Apr 14, 2017 5:28am

Game Day Prayer

"Dear Lord,

On this day, 2017 years ago, You paid the price for our sins, and you showed us what Love is. Continue to cover this program in love, and block out any negativity from the minds and ears of our daughters. Thank you for binding them together, and I ask that You continue to bring them closer with every second. Together, they are stronger, and each one brings a special talent and spirit to the team. Help them to celebrate each other and to lift each other up. You see their hard work, their tears, and their hearts. Reward their hard work, and give each one a nudge filled with Your glory. Fill them up with Your glory and build a FIREWALL around them that no one can cross." Amen

Apr 15, 2017 7:24am

Game Day Prayer

"Dear Lord,

Thank you for the blessings of today. Help our daughters to realize they are more than a number. Thank you for the grace they show every single time they come up to bat, field or throw a ball, or throw a pitch. Every time they blink, their performance is plastered on a big screen. They are more than a number to me...They are more than a number to You. They are precious in Your sight. Help them to realize how special they are and that they are precious to You. Thank you for using every experience to prepare them for the next challenge. When they look in the mirror, help them to see what YOU see. Set them apart, and give them the fruits of their labor." Amen

Apr 16, 2017 7:02am

Game Day Easter Prayer

"Dear Lord,

Thank you for making everything new and full of life. Help our daughters to celebrate life every day as they seek You and Your plan for their lives. Thank you for using softball as part of that plan. Help all of us to revisit what You did and to realize that in Your death and resurrection, You gave us forgiveness, freedom, and hope. I ask that You renew our daughters' and coaches' strength, courage, confidence, and hope today. Today is a new day, and all things are new in You." Amen

Apr 21, 2017 5:15am

Game Day Prayer

"Dear Lord,

Thank you for safe travels to South Carolina. As our daughters prepare for tonight's game, give them clarity, confidence, and peace of mind. Use this series to strengthen their faith and to help them to rely on You. Lift them up on eagles' wings, and help them walk right through any challenges they face." Amen

Apr 23, 2017 8:16am

Game Day Prayer

"Dear Lord,

As I read and listen to the folks that are so willing to tear down these young ladies and coaches, I am thankful that You are still here. You knew them before they were born, when they would take their first steps, what they would study in college, and You know who they will marry, where they will live, the lives that they will touch, and the day they will leave this earth. You are the master puzzle maker. We just see the pieces. You know how the puzzle will be put together. Sometimes we try to force the pieces but then, we find exactly where the piece belongs. Some pieces are dark; some are light. The pieces come in all shapes and sizes. As our daughters go out on the field today, help them realize that today is just one piece of the puzzle. Draw them to You, and give them the peace of mind and quiet confidence that only You can bring. Bring all of these pieces together to create a beautiful puzzle." Amen

Apr 26, 2017 3:19pm

Game Day Prayer

"Dear Lord,

Thank you for keeping Your promises. Thank you for answered and unanswered prayers. Continue to bind these young ladies in love. Give them confidence and peace of mind. Reward them for their hard work. May all that they do bring others to You." Amen

Apr 28, 2017 5:21am

Game Day Prayer

"Dear Lord,

Thank you for the blessings You have shown the AU players. Thank you for Your perfect timing and for binding these young ladies together in love. Thank you for the lifelong friendships and life lessons that have been made and learned for the seniors we celebrate this weekend. As they go out onto Jane B. Moore field for the last home series of the season, give them the courage to do what they have to do, and the hope for an extended season. May they have joy for what they are doing and play as if You are their Coach." Amen

Apr 29, 2017 8:10am

Game Day Prayer

"Dear Lord,

I want to praise You for the talent You have given our daughters. Thank you for using their talents as a vessel to get them to their destination. As we celebrate the seniors this weekend, I thank you for every hit, strike out, home run, walk, double play, put out, win and loss. I thank you for the moments our pitchers struck out the batters on a 3-2 count in the bottom of the seventh when we were ahead by one run and for the times they hit in the winning runs at the bottom of the seventh with a 3-2 count, and we were down by a run. I also want to thank you for the times is their lives when they may have missed an opportunity to hit in the winning run or get the batter to strike out. Thank you for the wins and the misses. The misses and losses gave them the drive to work harder, and the wins gave them hope. Continue to keep Your hand on their lives and help them to savor each moment today..it is filled with new opportunities." Amen

Apr 30, 2017 7:01am

On this day, the last day Kasey Cooper will put on orange and blue at Jane B. Moore field for a regular season home game, I am filled with pride of what she has accomplished as a softball player and a student. She is a remarkable athlete. I remember when she told me she wanted to play softball in college...I remember the prayer I prayed over her... That the coach that needed to see her would only see good things and for the coaches that didn't need to see her, she couldn't do enough. The Lord answered that prayer, and here we are nearing the end of four wonderful years at Auburn University. I am thankful for the times she has had here and for the friendships both she and we have made. I see you Kasey Cooper---the remarkable athlete and the even better person. I love you, Mom

Apr 30, 2017 7:23am

Game Day Prayer

"Dear Lord,

As we celebrate the seniors today, I want to thank you for directing their paths to Auburn University. These seniors have shared four years together. They've laughed, practiced, studied, cried, run, worked out, traveled, played, eaten, shopped, attended functions, worked camps, hosted recruits....together. There isn't much these young ladies haven't done together. They have learned to be sisters in Christ. They've loved each other and had fights....just like sisters. And just like sisters, they've learned to forgive each other and to stand strong as a family. Thank you for using softball to teach them what it means to be a family and to be united. As they go out on the field today, help their leadership to shine through. Thank you for seeing them through to this day, and thank you for the hope of tomorrow. Thank you for each one of these seniors. Please give them and all of the AU Tigers the fruits of their labor. May all that they do bring honor to You." Amen

May 03, 2017 5:24am

And it's another day of finals for our collegiate peeps.

"Dear Lord,

As our children and college friends go into another day of finals, renew their strength and stamina. Many are working off of coffee and soft drinks to stay up to get those last few hours of studying in. I ask that You multiply what little bit of sleep they have gotten so that they feel rested and ready to face the tasks that are in front of them...in this case 200 questions and a block of time. Give them clarity and peace of mind so that the answers come easily to them. Give them strong memories so that they can remember the content, the lecture, the formulas....whatever they are asked, they will know the answer. Being successful on these exams will get them closer to the destination You have planned for them, and I know that You will be with them today and this week. Help them feel Your presence." Amen

May 04, 2017 5:59am

Finals...Finals...more finals

"Dear Lord,

Please continue to multiply the little bit of sleep our college friends are getting as they prepare for the last two days of finals. I know they are weary and tired. Give them clear minds, calm spirits, and the stamina and strength to sit down and take another exam. Help the answers to come quickly and their confidence to get stronger with every question they answer. These exams are a step towards Your plan for their lives. Please surround them with Your presence this week. I praise You and thank you for walking before them and preparing them for today." Amen

May 05, 2017 5:13am

Finals...last day!

"Dear Lord,

Thank you for being with our college children and friends as they sit for final exams this week. As they go into this last round of examinations, renew their strength and minds. With each question they answer, increase their confidence. Clear their minds, and give them peace that only You can bring. Thank you for helping them feel Your presence as they get one step closer to the destination You have planned for them." Amen

May 05, 2017 5:22am

Game Day Prayer

"Dear Lord,

Thank you for safe travels to Tuscaloosa. Thank you for the opportunity to play at the Capstone in front of a group of fans that love their team as much as the Auburn fans love our team. As our daughters step onto the field, help them to focus on the little things...Softball 101. If they get the little things right, then good things will happen. Thank you for helping them get through finals this week...now all they have to do is play softball. Give them a carefree attitude and a sense of joy that only You can give. Continue to bind these young ladies together in love. A strand of 3 is not easily broken...a strand of 21 is rarely broken. Thank you for binding them together." Amen

May 06, 2017 8:10am

Happy Saturday!

"Dear Lord,

Thank you for being with our daughters. Every difficulty they face and conquer helps prepare them for the next battle. Thank you for helping them get through finals on coffee, soft drinks, and very little sleep -and then drive three hours to Tuscaloosa to face Bama and 4K very energetic Bama fans at Rhoads Stadium. As they go out today for Game 2, renew their strength. Renew their love of the game. Surround them with a wall of fire so that they only hear positives and instruction from the AU coaches and fans. Exams are over...thank you that they can play stress free and for the love of the game. Give them an extra spring in their step, spin on their pitches, gitty up in their throws, determination in their swings, and song in their hearts. May all that they do be a reflection of You in their hearts." Amen Game Time for Saturday was moved up to 7:00 central time.

May 07, 2017 6:43am

Game Day Prayer

"Dear Lord,

Thank you for the reminder yesterday and last night that our lives can change in an instant. Thank you for being able to see character revealed. Most of all thank you for Your amazing grace. As our daughters toe up for the last game of the Bama series, continue to bind them in love. Thank you for going in front of them preparing them for anything that may come their way. Keep them safe from injury, and continue to build a wall of fire around them so that they only hear the voices of their teammates, coaches, and words of encouragement. Give them the courage to trust their skills. There is nothing they can't do with You as their guiding force." Amen

May 10, 2017 5:21am

A prayer for Kasey and our softball friends around the country as they go into post season play. At the end of a day, softball is a game. Leave it all on the field. "Lord, keep them safe from injury, and may they play with all of the gifts You have given them. May they bring glory and honor to You with their words and actions." Amen

May 10, 2017 5:29am

"Dear Lord,

Please surround the AU players, fans, parents, and coaches as well as those of opposing teams with a safety net as they make their way to Knoxville, Tennessee to play in the SEC tournament. Clear their path so that anyone who sees them, hears them, talks to them, or thinks about them has you in their hearts. Thank you for using their talents to bring others to You. As they go into post season play, give them their best softball yet. Let their confidence build with each play, pitch, or swing of the bat. Help them to play above their abilities so that at the end of the day, people ask questions, and the answers lead to You. I ask that You multiply the fruits of their labor. You see them practice with their team. You see them practice without their team. You know their hearts. Thank you for allowing them to live their testimony playing a game they love." Amen

May 11, 2017 5:17am

Game Day Prayer

"Dear Lord,

Thank you for today and for another chance for our daughters tighten up the laces on their cleats and to button up those jerseys. Continue to draw them together as one unit. You have been preparing them for today since the day they were born. Help them to go out onto the field with confidence, composure, grace, and joy. Confidence will help them get back into that batter's box or get ready to pitch when they might have missed a spot pitching or just missed a pitch batting. Composure and grace will help them keep smiles on their faces when an official's call may have missed the mark. Joy will help them remember why they started playing the game in the first place. Give them a warrior's heart, and help them use every last ounce of energy they have to play their best softball and to bring honor to You." Amen

May 12, 2017 2:28pm

Game Day Prayer

"Dear Lord,

Thank you for the blessings of today. Thank you for going in front of our daughters giving them experiences to prepare them for today. Help them to always look ahead. Help them to have short memories and the will to battle until the last out. Keep the players from all teams safe as they play the game they love. Build a wall of fire around them so that they only hear positive words and they only say positive words to each other. May all that they do bring honor to You." Amen

May 13, 2017 7:33am

Get your umbrellas ready.

"Heavenly Father,

Thank you for continuing to rain down your blessings on the AU softball players and coaches. You are a God of 'You can do that' and a God of restoration. Help our players break through the artificial limits they have set in their own lives. Help them see that You are limitless." Amen

May 19, 2017 4:47am

Game Day Prayer

"Dear Lord,

Thank you for HOPE. Hope allows us to anxiously wait for an expected outcome. As our daughters go into today's game, let them do so with hope and excitement. Thank you for renewing their passion and for helping them remember why they play the game. Thank you for the smiles and giggles that abound and for the joyous hearts that they have. They've worked all season for This season. Thank you for renewing their strength and their spirit. Help the pitchers to pitch so sharply that they could be blindfolded and still hit their spots. Help the fielders to anticipate and respond to plays like a seasoned chess player---they know exactly where the ball is going to be hit...and they will be there. Help the hitters to see the ball well and to hit as if they were in the backyard with friends---with confidence and joy and an attitude of, 'Go ahead…give me your best pitch…I'm hitting it.' Help our daughters to play above their ability and to play with such passion that there is no doubt to observers that You have a hand on this program and on these players. They are a new team with a new drive and a new season. Thank you for new opportunities to use softball as a platform to display the talents You have given our daughters and as a starting point to bring others to you. Keep players from all teams safe during this tournament, and help us to be gracious hosts and hostesses." Amen

May 20, 2017 5:45am

Game Day Prayer

"Dear Lord,

Thank you for the blessings of today and for the opportunity to watch our daughters play a game that they love---a game that is part of the plan You have for their lives. Thank you for continuing to draw them together in love. Keep the game simple for them. See the ball....catch the ball. Catch the ball...throw the ball. See the ball...hit the ball. Get the pitch call, pitch to the glove. Just like life, sometimes, we over think over complicate, when others can recognize and say...'You are making this too hard.' Thank you for the coaches in our daughters' lives who can simplify the game for our daughters. Thank You for being the ultimate Simplifier...You go before our daughters and prepare their paths. Continue to put joy in their hearts and laughter on their lips. Help them to trust what they have learned and to step out with confidence and HOPE with great excitement and anticipation of great things to come. Put a wall of fire around players from all teams to protect them from injury. Help the AU fans, parents, players, and coaches be gracious hosts and hostesses. May all that we do bring honor and glory to You." Amen

May 21, 2017 7:18am

Game Day Prayer

"Dear Lord,

Thank you for the blessings of today. Thank you for one more day of Auburn softball----One more day for our daughters to play the game they love with the talents You have given to them. Thank you for being a God of restoration. Help our daughters to see what YOU SEE. Your child---clothed in dignity and strength---with a body that is beautifully and wonderfully made--with a spirit of boldness. Help our daughters to be mindful of the fact that they are YOUR children. Help them to play with the quiet confidence and strength that only You can give to them. Close their ears and eyes so that they only hear and see positives. Thank You for answered prayers. They lift each other up, and they are playing as one team. Continue to keep them safe, and help them to have a warrior's heart, and to fight until the last out is made. Build a wall of fire to keep all of the players safe and free from injury. At the end of the day, help others to know without any doubt that You have Your hand on these young ladies and the AU softball coaches. May all that they do bring honor and glory to You. Help them play for You." Amen

May 26, 2017 5:16am

Game Day Prayer

"Dear Lord,

Thank you for Your continued blessings. Thank you for giving our daughters the opportunity to play softball and to use the game of softball as a platform to start conversations about their lives and You. Many of them were told at some point growing up that they were not quick enough, not big enough, not tall enough...not...to play softball at the collegiate level, yet here they are. Thank you for taking them where they were and filling in the voids with Your strength and Your Spirit. They are more than enough because of You. Today, as they step onto the Jane B. Moore Field, give them confidence and assurance that they are 'more than enough' to face any opponent." Amen

May 27, 2017 8:22am

Game Day Prayer

"Dear Lord,

Thank you for having already decided the outcome of today. Thank you for allowing our daughters to put on an Auburn University softball jersey today. As our daughters prepare for Game 2 against Oklahoma, thank you for having them right where they need to be. Help them to realize that they are the only ones that can make the outstanding plays on defense, the only ones that can hit the ball, and the only ones that can pitch the ball. You put them in the right conditions for those plays to be made, but they have to make them. It takes courage to give it your all--to go all out. Father, give them the courage to step out and step up to the task You have laid in front of them. Today help them leave it all on the field so that when the last out is made, they can say, 'I gave it my all.'" Amen

May 27, 2017 2:59pm

Today is the last day Kasey wore an Auburn University softball uniform. I was blessed to see her first game and her last as an AU Tiger. So proud of the young lady she has become. War Eagle, Kasey. You gave your best to AU softball.

Jun 12, 2017 5:56am

"Dear Lord,

Keep the members of Team USA and their coaches safe as they make their way to training camp. May all who see them, hear them, talk to them, or think about them have You in their hearts. Give Your angels charge over them as they begin the summer season. May others get a glimpse of Your greatness as they see them and meet them. Father, bless them." Amen

Jun 19, 2017 6:42pm

Cooper quote...

"Just because folks try to cover you up with dirt doesn't stop you from being a diamond."

Jul 06, 2017 7:09am

One of my favorite question and answers from Faith Night was, "How do stay positive when you're having a bad night?" Two responses, "Well, you know if I'm 0/2 for the night, I can't get down. I have to get back in there. If I am 1/3 for the night, that's a really good night." The other response, "We all chose a team sport." I would say, "Team USA plays as ONE TEAM." Keep an eye on this bunch---there are many championships in their future.

Jul 13, 2017 5:24am

I have been around softball my entire life...as an observer, player, and coach. We always hear and say, "Trust the process." Let's turn it up a notch, "Trust God." When I look back over my own life, Mr. Perfect didn't call back...I later married my prince of 31 years. I just couldn't get past the third year accounting courses in college, so I changed my major to English and Spanish--two majors. I later found out I have dyslexia...Accounting probably would not have been my best career choice. I also had the chance to teach and coach high schoolers for over a decade and fought...and I do mean fought...to bring softball AND volleyball to Dothan City Schools. Both of my daughters played both sports, and both received softball scholarships...as many other talented athletes have since 1989. Later, I moved to a new school system and after a promise was broken to me, I left on principle; in fact; I left the K-12 environment for a private company. I found myself working at a nuclear plant in a training academy...teaching our teachers. My experiences as a coach and educator before I arrived in a work environment that is 90% male definitely prepared me for my current career. I wanted to be a principal---to make a difference when I was a teacher. I get to do that now as a training manager. The difference is I get to impact not only the lives of the people I work with every day, I get to impact an entire industry both in the US and abroad. So, why do I share this today? I was lead to---so whoever this is for...God's not finished. He's working on you like He has worked on me my entire life. His plan is better than our plan.

Sep 14, 2017 5:45am

Very proud of these talented athletes, and happy they will be back in the USA today sporting a new piece of GOLD jewelry. Congratulations Eagles!

Dec 31, 2017 7:33am

"Dear Lord,

Please bestow travel mercies and Your hand of protection on Kasey Cooper and all of the Team USA hopefuls as they make their way to Clearwater for tryouts this week. May all who see them, talk to them, hear them, or think about them have You in their hearts." Amen

Jan 01, 2018 6:45pm

Today was the first day of tryouts for Team USA softball hopefuls. Over 60 players will play 6 games, and then on Friday...or Saturday, the roster will be named. These young ladies are chasing a dream—--many have dreamed of having USA across their chest since they were old enough to say, "USA."

They have worked in the rain, the snow, the turf, the dirt, the grass,—-all year round. They chose to work for the chance to try out for Team USA. The time they've been working for is now—-today—this week.

All the best to Kasey Cooper, current, and former Team USA players and current and former collegiate and professional teammates—-In the words of one of my favorite coaches, "Act like you've been here before." I'm so proud of all of you. Never look back, and don't trust the bounce! GO TEAM USA!

Jan 02, 2018 7:28am

Day 2 of Team USA tryouts is about to start:) It's a blustery 40 degrees in Clearwater:) This group of athletes will be groomed to be part of the 2020 Olympic softball team. Prayers for all to play their best softball, no injuries, a warrior spirit, and wisdom for the selection committee members. Iron sharpens iron…..Go TEAM USA.

Jan 07, 2018 7:28am

It takes a village. Thank you to our softball family—-USA, AU, Scrapyard Dawgs, Fury Nation, Dothan, friends, and family for supporting Kasey Cooper. Prayers, practices, workouts, fields—-can't be done alone. Cooper, party of ###. You know who you are. Thank you!

ABOUT THE AUTHOR

Peppi Cooper is a coach, mother, wife, and long-time fan of women's softball. She fought and won the battle to have softball instituted in Dothan City Schools in Dothan, Alabama, and went on to be the first head coach at Northview High School. She also coached for both recreational and travel softball programs. Both of her daughters played softball in Dothan City Schools and later in Division 1 colleges. Her oldest daughter, Kortney Cooper, played at Troy University. Her youngest daughter, Kasey Cooper, played at Auburn University and for the USA Women's National Softball Team. Both she and her husband, Jeff, are still involved with softball as mentors to coaches, parents, and players. You can usually find the Coopers either on a softball field or in the bleachers cheering.

Printed in the United States
By Bookmasters